FIFA Museum Collection

1000 years of Football
1000 ans de Football
1000 años de Fútbol
1000 Jahre Fußball

edition q

Le fait que le football compte des millions d'adeptes à travers le monde relève de la fascination qui elle-même comprend de nombreuses facettes ayant pour la plupart toutes déjà été analysées et documentées.

Pour de nombreuses personnes, cette fascination est fondée sur le pont que le football jette entre le passé, le présent et le futur. Les traditions du jeu ne remontent pas à hier et sont chéries non seulement par ceux qui les vivent mais également par ceux qui apprécient que les valeurs du présent soient établies par celles du passé.

C'est ainsi que la FIFA est enchantée de pouvoir jouer son rôle de garant de l'héritage du football en acquérant une partie du FIFA Museum Collection. Etant donné que l'histoire du sport le plus populaire au monde est bien trop vaste et trop variée pour pouvoir tenir dans un livre, les images de la Collection reflètent l'expression de cet héritage pertinent et succint.

Dans ces pages, des sujets de la collection évoqueront des émotions empreintes à la fois de nostalgie, de surprise et d'enchantement. Elles rapèleront peut-être des souvenirs à moitié oubliés, ou raviveront les mémoires embrumées par le temps. Elles surprendront beaucoup d'entre vous par leur beauté, leur humour ou par l'evocation des récits du passé. Elles aideront à rétablir le contexte du passé et à former ainsi la base pour une meilleure compréhension de la destinée de notre sport.

Toutefois et par dessus tout, ces pages réjouiront aussi bien l'obvervateur fortuit que l'amoureux du football ou encore le profane désireux d'en savoir plus sur le jeu. Quelle que soit la motivation qui vous pousse à feuilleter les pages qui suivent, nous espérons sincèrement qu'elles seront à votre goût.

Dr. João Havelange
Président de la FIFA

Existen muchas facetas en la fascinación que despierta el fútbol en millones de adeptos en el mundo, y muchas de ellas han sido frecuentemente analizadas y documentadas.

Para muchas personas, esta fascinación se basa en el eslabón que el fútbol forja entre el pasado, el presente y el futuro. Las tradiciones del juego tienen orígenes profundos y las estiman no sólo aquellos que las viven sino también aquellos que aprecian el hecho de que los valores del presente están asentados en los del pasado.

De esta manera, la FIFA está encantada de poder desempeñar su papel de protectora de la herencia del fútbol adquiriendo una parte de la FIFA Museum Collection. En vista de que la historia del deporte más popular del mundo es muy extensa y muy variada para poder ser contada en un libro, las imágenes de la colección reflejan la expresión de esta herencia sucinta.

En estas páginas, los temas de la colección evocarán emociones mixtas de nostalgia, sorpresa y encanto. Evocarán quizás recuerdos medio olvidados, o revivirán memorias oscurecidas por el transcurso del tiempo. Les sorprenderá a muchos por su belleza, humor y por la sutileza de las reliquias del pasado. Estas ayudarán a restablecer el contexto del ayer y formarán así la base para una mejor comprensión del desarrollo de nuestro deporte.

Sobre todo, y sin embargo, estas páginas darán un gran placer tanto al observador benévolo como al amante del fútbol o incluso al profano deseoso de saber más sobre el juego. Cualquiera sea la motivación que le empuje a hojear las siguientes páginas, esperamos sinceramente que disfrute de ellas.

Dr. João Havelange
Presidente de la FIFA

Die Faszination, die der Fußball auf viele Menschen in der ganzen Welt ausübt, hat zahlreiche Aspekte, wobei die meisten schon häufig analysiert und dokumentiert worden sind.

Für viele Menschen beruht diese Faszination auf der Verbindung zwischen Vergangenheit, Gegenwart und Zukunft, welche der Fußball schafft. Die Traditionen des Spiels sind tief verankert und werden von jenen, die sie selbst geschaffen haben, ebenso gepflegt wie von denen, die es schätzen, daß die Werte der Gegenwart durch die Werte der Vergangenheit bestimmt werden.

Die FIFA war daher hocherfreut, mit dem Erwerb der FIFA Museum Collection ihrer Rolle als Bewahrerin der Fußballtradition gerecht werden zu können. Die Geschichte der beliebtesten Sportart der Welt ist zu umfangreich und besitzt zu viele Facetten, als daß sie in einem Band Platz finden könnte. Die Ausstellungsstücke der Collection vermitteln aber ein so vollständiges und authentisches Bild, wie es nur möglich ist.

Auf den folgenden Seiten werden einige der Exponate nicht nur nostalgische Gefühle wecken, sondern auch Überraschung und Fazination auslösen. Halbvergessenes wird wiedererwachen und vage Erinnerungen werden ins rechte Licht gerückt. Viele Betrachter werden überrascht sein von der Schönheit, dem Humor und der Qualität dieser Relikte, die uns die Vergangenheit etwas näher bringen und so das Verständnis für die Entwicklung unseres Sports fördern werden.

In erster Linie sollen die folgenden Seiten dem geneigten Betrachter wie auch dem eingefleischten Fußballfan oder dem sportgeschichtlich Interessierten Vergnügen bereiten. Aus welchem Grund Sie dieses Buch auch zur Hand genommen haben, wir hoffen sehr, daß es Ihnen gefallen wird.

Dr. João Havelange
FIFA-Präsident

There are many facets to the fascination that football holds on millions of people throughout the world, and most of these have been frequently analysed and documented.

For many people, this fascination is founded in the link that football forges between the past, the present and the future. The traditions of the game run deep, and are cherished not only by those who lived them at first hand but also by those who appreciate that the values of the present are set by the values of the past.

Thus FIFA was delighted to be able to play its role as a protector of football's heritage by acquiring joint ownership of the FIFA Museum Collection. While the history of the world's most popular sport is simply too vast and too varied to be comprehensively recounted or portrayed in any one volume, the images of the Collection are as pertinent and succinct an expression of this heritage as one is likely to find.

In these pages, items from the Collection will evoke mixed emotions of nostalgia, surprise and enlightenment. They will recall half-forgotten souvenirs, maybe, or serve to correct memories grown hazy through the passage of time; they will surprise many by the beauty, the humour or the sophistication of the relics of the past; and they will help set the context for the past and thus form the basis for a better understanding of our sport's destiny.

Above all, however, these pages will give pleasure, to the casual observer as well as to dedicated lovers of football or the game's more serious students. Whatever your motive for looking through the pages that follow, we sincerely hope you will enjoy them.

Dr. Joâo Havelange
President of FIFA

Mille ans d'histoire du Football

Nous disons souvent que notre avenir se nourrit de notre passé. Cette affirmation est sans doute fondée mais elle ne s'applique pas à tous les aspects de la vie.

Comme les médias et les techniques de communication modernes se développent à une vitesse que même les pays à la pointe du progrès estiment parfois ahurissante, il peut apparaître confortable et sécurisant de se replonger dans les images familières du passé. Même si ce passé est antérieur à notre naissance, les témoignages qu'il nous a légués ont bercé nos années de formation et impressionné nos esprits de manière indélébile.

Peut-être est-ce là aussi une aspiration nostalgique à une simplicité que symbolise un temps révolu, une aspiration à une époque que nous qualifions non sans raison d'âge de l'innocence.

Les oeuvres de la FIFA Museum Collection offrent aux nostalgiques quelques raisons de rêver. Assemblées par Harry Langton, un Anglais passionné de football, elles constituent le témoignage le plus complet sur l'histoire du ballon rond. D'une grande richesse, cette collection séduit même les esprits déjà tournés vers le 21ème siècle.

Joseph S. Blatter
Secrétaire Général, FIFA

Mil años de historia del Fútbol

Frecuentemente se dice que nuestro futuro yace en nuestras raíces. Tal vez sea cierto en algunos aspectos de la vida, pero no en todos.

A medida que avanza la moderna era de la comunicación – a un paso tal que incluso deja perplejos a muchos de los que vivimos en las partes más desarrolladas tecnológicamente del mundo –, parece que aún es posible hallar cierta intimidad y seguridad al recordar imágenes familiares del pasado, imágenes que ya existían y acompañaron nuestros primeros años de formación, dejando huellas indelebles en nuestro ser.

Quizá añoremos esa simplicidad del pasado, aquella época a la que a menudo nos referimos, y con razón, como los años de la inocencia.

Sin duda existe también un enorme e inherente anhelo nostálgico en las piezas que conforman la FIFA Museum Collection. Esta muestra artística del deporte, reunida y documentada cariñosamente por Harry Langton, un inglés apasionado del fútbol, despliega la más extensa colección de recuerdos del fútbol, un caleidoscopio que estimulará la imaginación incluso de los espíritus ya orientados hacia el siglo XXI.

Joseph S. Blatter
Secretario General, FIFA

Tausend Jahre Fußballgeschichte

Oft wird gesagt, die Gegenwart schöpfe aus der Vergangenheit. Diese Aussage entbehrt bestimmt nicht einer gewissen Grundlage, sie trifft aber nicht auf alle Lebensbereiche zu.

Da sich die Medien und die modernen Kommunikationsmittel in einem Tempo entwickeln, das manchmal selbst den führenden Ländern atemberaubend erscheint, kann es bequem und beruhigend sein, in den altbekannten Bildern der Vergangenheit zu schwelgen. Denn obschon diese Vergangenheit vor unserer Geburt stattfand, so hat sie doch unsere Jugend geprägt und unauslöschliche Eindrücke hinterlassen.

Vielleicht ist es auch die Sehnsucht nach der Einfachheit einer vergangenen Zeit, die Sehnsucht nach einer Epoche, die für uns nicht ohne Grund das Zeitalter der Unschuld symbolisiert.

Die Ausstellungsstücke der FIFA Museum Collection – von Harry Langton, einem vom Fußball faszinierten Engländer, gesammelt – regen Nostalgiker zum Träumen an, stellen sie doch das umfassendste Zeugnis der Geschichte unseres Sports dar. In ihrer Größe und Bedeutung zieht die Sammlung aber sogar jene an, deren Geist bereits auf das 21. Jahrhundert ausgerichtet ist.

Joseph S. Blatter
FIFA-Generalsekretär

A THOUSAND YEARS OF FOOTBALL HISTORY

Our future, it is frequently said, lies in our past. That may be so in some walks of life, but not in all.

As the modern media age of communications develops at a rate which many of us even in the most technologically developed parts of the world sometimes find baffling, there appears to be comfort and safety to be found in clinging more closely to the familiar images of the past - a past which may even pre-date our own lives, but whose images were there to accompany our early formative years and leave behind indelible impressions.

Maybe there is also a nostalgic yearning for a certain simplicity which is implied in a bygone age, the age not unreasonably also often referred to as that of innocence.

Certainly there is a huge nostalgic appeal inherent in the artefacts that form the FIFA Museum Collection. Lovingly assembled and documented by Harry Langton, an Englishman with a passion for the game, which expresses itself in the world's most comprehensive collection of football memorabilia, the collection never fails to catch the imagination even of the most progressive 21st century man.

Joseph S. Blatter
General Secretary, FIFA

Introduction

Football began somewhere in the mists of antiquity with glimpses of an ancient game in China, among the Toltecs, the Ancient Greeks, the clans of Scotland.

The rules, if there were any, varied from nation to nation, region to region, village to village but the common elements were in place an age ago – a ball, men and the desire for play and competition.

There are many signs in history of the importance of football. An English king banned the game because he feared his bowmen were spending too much time away from archery practice in preparation for war against France.

Oliver Cromwell played football at Cambridge University in the early 1600s and said the only man he feared on the football field was one John Wheelright – who later took his family and his game to America, where his portrait now hangs in the State House; looking down on Boston Common where the first football game was played in the New World. There are links between British football and Il Calcio of Italy in the Renaissance writings of an English head master in the years between 1561 and 1608. There is a legend recorded in a 17th century "Statistical Account of Scotland" that Football "had its origins in the days of chivalry, when it is alleged that an Italian who came into Scotland challenged all the parishes in the neighbourhood of Scone. (...) Scone accepted, beat the foreigner and in consequence the game was instituted."

But it was not until the 19th century that a group of men met in London to bring some order to the varieties of football being played and set down the Laws of the Game of Association Football. Others, then and later, preferred a different game and so began Rugby Football, divided later into Rugby Union and Rugby League, and leading, through time and adaptation, to American Football and Australian Rules.

It is, of course, the Association game – our football – which has become the sporting phenomenon of the world, reaching into every corner of humankind.

However, if football began in antiquity, the FIFA Museum Collection, this most magnificent record of the past, began with a 5 shilling purchase of a small print in the 1950s; bought as a present by Mrs Ann Langton for her husband Harry Langton who went on to assemble paintings and prints, balls and boots, toys and games, ceramics and sculptures which show how deeply people felt about their game long before the age of communication made the world's delight obvious to all.

The FIFA Museum Collection is the result of those long years of Football's past and also the long years of care and devotion and patience of Harry Langton who has sometimes characterized the Collection as "an accident" and said that sometimes objects became known to him in such strange ways it was if "they wanted to be found for posterity". If so, it was a happy accident and it is certain that other objects will appear ... because no matter how full and beautiful, the FIFA Museum Collection is not complete any more than football itself is complete.

As the game grows, as our future becomes the past, the thread which links humanity through football will remain intact because of the FIFA Museum Collection.

Introduction

Le football apparut à partir de quelques éléments d'un ancien jeu chinois, parmi les Toltecs, les Grecs anciens et les clans écossais, vers le milieu de l'antiquité.

Les règles, si tant est qu'il y en ait eu, variaient d'une nation à l'autre, d'une région à l'autre, d'un village à l'autre, mais des éléments communs étaient déjà en place: une balle, des hommes et l'envie de jouer ainsi que l'émulation de la compétition.

Il existe de nombreux signes au cours de l'histoire illustrant l'importance du football. Un roi anglais interdit le jeu, car il craignait que ses soldats ne consacrent que trop peu de temps au tir à l'arc, et ne se préparent pas suffisamment à la guerre contre la France.

Oliver Cromwell jouait au football à l'université de Cambridge au début du 17 ème siècle, et disait que le seul homme qu'il craignait sur un terrain de football était un certain John Wheelright. Ce dernier emmena quelques années plus tard sa famille et ce jeu aux Etats Unis, où son portrait est encore suspendu au Parlement, surplombant Boston Common, parc où se joua le premier match de football sur le sol du Nouveau Monde.

Les écrits d'un proviseur anglais de la Renaissance daté des années 1561 à 1608, rapportent l'existence de liens entre le football britannique et l'«Il Calcio» italien. On retrouve une légende dans un «recueil de récits d'Ecosse» du 17ème siècle, qui prétend que les origines du football «remontaient à l'époque de la chevalerie, lorsqu'un Italien venu en Ecosse défia toutes les paroisses aux alentours de Scone. Elles acceptèrent, battirent l'étranger et en conséquence instaurèrent le jeu.»

Mais ce n'est pas avant le 19ème siècle, qu'un groupe d'hommes se réunit à Londres afin d'uniformiser les différentes formes de jeu et de fixer les règles de l'Association du Football. Certains se détournèrent alors du football et lui préférèrent un autre sport. Ainsi naquît le football-rugby qui se scinda ultérieurement en Union du Rugby et en Ligue du Rugby, avant d'évoluer au grè du temps et des adaptations, en football américain et en football australien. Ce fut bien sûr l'Association du Football, c'est à dire notre forme de football, qui devint un phénomène sportif mondial, atteignant les coins les plus reculés de l'humanité.

Cependant, si le football naquît dès l'antiquité, la collection du musée de la FIFA, ce magnifique témoignage du passé, ne commença qu'avec l'achat pour cinq shillings d'une petite image dans les années cinquante; un petit présent de Madame Ann Langton à son époux Harry Langton, qui se mit alors à rassembler peintures et images, ballons et chaussures, jouets et jeux, céramiques et sculptures illustrant l'intensité et la profondeurs des liens qui unissaient les gens à leur jeu, bien avant que l'âge de la communication ne rende ce plaisir accessible à tous.

La collection du musée de la FIFA, est le résultats de ces longues années qui ont fait l'histoire du football, mais aussi de ces longues années d'attention, de dévotion et de patience durant lesquelles Harry Langton qualifia parfois cette collection «d'accidentelle», et révéla que certains objets lui étaient parvenus de manière si étrange, qu'ils semblaient «vouloir passer à la postérité».

S'il en est ainsi, ce fut un heureux accident, et il est fort probable que d'autres objets apparaîtront encore ... car même riche et belle, la collection du musée de la FIFA n'est pas plus achevée que le football lui-même. Alors que le jeu s'étend, que notre futur devient passé, le souffle qui lie l'humanité au football demeurera intact grâce à la collection du musée de la FIFA.

Introducción

El fútbol tuvo origen en algún punto nebuloso de la antiguedad que, mirando al pasado, tiene que ver con juegos practicados en la antigua China, entre los Toltecas, la antigua Grecia y los clanes de Escocia.

Las reglas, si alguna vez existieron, variaban de país en país, región en región, aldea en aldea, pero los elementos comunes se establecieron hace un siglo: una pelota, hombres y el deseo de jugar y competir.

En la historia se encuentran muchas huellas que atestiguan la importancia del fútbol. Un rey inglés, por ejemplo, prohibió el juego, porque tenía miedo que sus tiradores de arco pasaran demasiado tiempo jugándolo y que no asistieran a las prácticas de tiro con arco, útiles en su preparación para la guerra contra Francia. Oliver Cromwell jugó al fútbol en la universidad de Cambridge a comienzos del siglo diecisiete y dijo que la única persona a la cual temía en el campo de juego, era un tal John Wheelright. Éste, años más tarde, levó a su familia y al juego a Norteamérica, donde ahora cuelga su retrato en el Capitolio, mirando hacia Boston Common, lugar en que se llevó a cabo el primer partido de fútbol en el Nuevo Mundo.

Existe relación entre el fútbol británico y el calcio italiano, según los escritos renacentistas de un director de colegio inglés entre los años 1561 y 1608. Hay una leyenda mencionada en los "Informes Estadísticos de Escocia" del siglo XVII, según la cual el fútbol "tuvo su orígen en tiempos de los caballeros, cuando un italiano vino a Escocia para desafiar al fútbol a todas las comarcas vecinas a Scone. (...) Scone acceptó, ganó al extranjero y como consecuencia quedó instituido el juego".

Pero fue recién en el siglo XIX, cuando un grupo de señores se reunió en Londres para poner algo de orden en las diferentes variedades de fútbol que se practicaba y establecer las Reglas del Juego de la Federación de Fútbol. Otros, en ese tiempo y después, prefirieron un juego diferente y así se inició el Rugby, que después se dividió en la Federación de Rugby y la Liga de Rugby, dando origen con el tiempo y según las adaptaciones al fútbol americano y al fútbol australiano. Nuestro fútbol, el juego de la Federación, es por supuesto, el que se convirtió en el fenómeno deportivo mundial, que llega a todos los rincones del planeta.

Aunque el fútbol empezó en la antigüedad, la colección del museo de la FIFA, la muestra más importante del pasado, empieza con un pequeño cartel adquirido por cinco chelines en los años 50. Dicho cartel fue comprado por la señora Ann Langton para ser regalado a su esposo, Harry Langton, quien quería comenzar a coleccionar cuadros, carteles, pelotas, botines, jugetes, juegos, cerámicas y esculturas alusivas, los que muestran cuán profundamente impresionada con el juego se encontraba la gente mucho antes de que la era de la comunicación hizo visible para todos este encanto mundial. La colección del museo de la FIFA es el resultado de todos estos largos años del pasado del fútbol y también de los muchos años del cuidado, de la paciencia y devoción de Harry Langton. Él a veces denominaba la colección como "un accidente" y decía que la existencia de muchos objetos llegó a su conocimiento por caminos tan extraños que parecía como "si quisieran ser encontrados en la posteridad". Si esto fue así, se trata de un feliz accidente, que ciertamente permitirá que muchos otros objetos sigan apareciendo ... porque por más grande y hermosa que sea, la colección del museo de la FIFA no estará nunca completa, como nunca el propio fútbol detendrá su desarrollo. Así como el juego crece, y así como nuestro futuro se convierte en pasado, así tambíen, el aliento que une a la humanidad a través del fútbol permanecerá intacto debido a la colección del museo de la FIFA.

Einleitung

Die Anfänge des Fußballs reichen in ferne Vergangenheit zurück, mit uralten Ballspielen in China, bei den Tolteken, im antiken Griechenland, bei den schottischen Clans. Die Regeln, sofern es überhaupt welche gab, waren von Nation zu Nation, von Region zu Region, von Siedlung zu Siedlung verschieden, doch bereits in dieser Frühzeit gab es das einigende Band – einen Ball, Spieler und das Verlangen nach Spiel und Wettstreit. Für die Bedeutung des Fußballs schon damals gibt es vielfältige Belege. Ein englischer König verbot das Spiel, weil er fürchtete, daß seine Bogenschützen damit zu stark von ihren Vorbereitungen auf den Krieg gegen Frankreich abgelenkt werden würden. Oliver Cromwell spielte in seinen Cambridger Studentenjahren zu Beginn des 17. Jahrhunderts Fußball, der einzige Mann, den er auf dem Feld fürchtete, war ein gewisser John Wheelright – der später das Spiel nach Amerika mitbrachte, wo heute noch sein Porträt im State House von Boston hängt und auf den Platz hinabschaut, der seinerzeit das erste Fußballspiel in der Neuen Welt erlebte.

Aus der Zeit der Renaissance sind Verbindungen zwischen dem britischen Football und dem italienischen Il Calcio überliefert. Ein „Statistischer Bericht von Schottland" aus dem 17. Jahrhundert überliefert die Legende, Football habe „seinen Ursprung in den Zeiten des Rittertums, da ein Italiener nach Schottland kam und alle Gemeinden rund um Scone herausforderte. (...) Die Männer von Scone waren einverstanden, schlugen den Ausländer und fortan war das Spiel eingeführt."

Doch erst im 19. Jahrhundert sollte sich eine Gruppe von Männern in London zusammenfinden, um Ordnung in die unterschiedlichen Arten des Fußballspiels zu bringen und die Regeln für den künftigen Association Football festzulegen. Andere bevorzugten ein anderes Spiel, so nahm der Rugby Football seinen Anfang, aus dem sich im Laufe der Zeit auch der American Football sowie die besondere australische Variante entwickelten.

Zum Massen-Phänomen indes wurde der Association Football – unser heutiger Fußball –, gespielt bis in den letzten Winkel der Erde.

Fußball nahm seinen Anfang in grauer Vorzeit. Die Geschichte der FIFA Museum Collection – einer großartigen Dokumentation zur Vergangenheit des Spiels – begann kurz nach 1950 mit dem Kauf eines Druckes für 5 Shilling; erworben von Mrs. Ann Langton als Geschenk für ihren Gatten Harry Langton. Dieser baute in der Folgezeit mit wachsender Begeisterung seine einmalige Sammlung auf: Gemälde und Drucke, Bälle und Fußballschuhe, Spielzeug und Spiele, Keramik und Skulpturen; allesamt Stücke, die zeigen, wie begeistert die Menschen vom Fußballspiel waren, lange bevor das Medienzeitalter diese Begeisterung weltweit vermittelte.

Die FIFA Museum Collection ist gleichermaßen Resultat jener langen Jahre der Geschichte des Fußballs als auch der vielen Jahre Hingebung und Geduld von Harry Langton. Er hat seine Sammlung einmal als „Zufall" bezeichnet und dazu gesagt, von manchen Objekten habe er auf so seltsame Weise Kenntnis erhalten, daß er fast glaubte, „sie wollten wohl erst in der Ewigkeit aufgespürt werden".

Wenn das so ist, so war es ein glücklicher Zufall, und wir können davon ausgehen, daß weitere Objekte auftauchen werden. Denn: So prachtvoll und umfangreich die FIFA Museum Collection auch ist – sie ist nicht vollständiger als der Fußball selbst. In dem Maße, da das Spiel sich weiter ausbreitet, da unsere Zukunft zur Vergangenheit wird, wird auch das Band, das die Menschheit mittels Fußball verbindet, weiter intakt bleiben – nicht zuletzt durch die FIFA Museum Collection.

1 Ancient History
Histoire ancienne
Historia antigua
Frühgeschichte

Football and Handball games reach back to the first steps of the human race. Over thousands of years, ancient communities introduced rules to their elementary play of kicking and throwing. Games also embellished religious or tribal festivals.

The Chinese played Football games at least 3000 years ago. It is suspected strongly that the shadowy Celtic nations of Europe, and the Vikings, had rather nasty Football ceremonies. In South and Central America a game called "Tlatchi" once flourished. The Ancient Greeks and the Romans used Football games to sharpen warriors for battle. Roman games such as Harpastum or Paganica , which all had elements of kicking or running with the ball, spread Europe-wide with their empire's armies. Here are the European seeds of what Football eventually became in the 19th Century and what it remains today.

Le football et le handball remontent presque aux origines de l'humanité. Durant des millénaires, les communautés primitives introduisirent des règles à leurs jeux élémentaires de lancer et de frapper. Ces jeux agrémentaient les fêtes religieuses ou tribales. Les Chinois jouaient déjà au football il y a trois mille ans. Il est très vraisemblable, que les nations celtiques d'Europe que l'on connaît mal, ainsi que les Vikings, pratiquaient un football rituel assez violent. En Amérique du Sud et en Amérique Centrale fleurit jadis un jeu nommé «Tlatchi». Les jeux romains tels le Harpastum ou le Paganica, comprennant tous deux des éléments de frappe et de course avec une balle, se répandirent à travers toute l'Europe avec les armées de l'empire. Ces jeux romains constituèrent les racines européennes du football, à partir desquelles apparut finalement le football du 19ème siècle, puis le football contemporain.

Los orígenes de los juegos de balompié y de balonmano se remontan a los primeros pasos de la raza humana. Durante miles de años, comunidades antiguas introdujeron reglas en sus juegos elementales de patear y lanzar. Los partidos también adornaban las ceremonias religiosas y tribales. Los chinos jugaron partidos de balompié hace por lo menos 3000 años. Se tiene la fuerte sospecha que las naciones celtas de Europa y los vikingos tenían ceremonias bastante salvajes de balompié. En Sudamérica y en Centroamérica alguna vez floreció un juego llamado "Tlatchi".

Los antiguos griegos y los romanos utilizaron los juegos de balompié como entrenamiento de los soldados para la batalla. Juegos romanos como Harpastum o Paganica, que tenían elementos de patear y correr con la pelota, se difundieron a todo lo ancho de Europa por los ejercitos imperiales. Ahí están las semillas europeas de lo que finalmente se convirtió en el fútbol del siglo XIX y en el de hoy en día.

Fußball- und Handballspiele reichen zurück bis zu den ersten Schritten der menschlichen Rasse. Über Jahrtausende entwickelten dann die Gemeinschaften des Altertums Regeln für ihr elementares Spiel des Kickens und Werfens mit dem Ball, das auch Bestandteil religiöser oder gemeinschaftlicher Feste war.

In China fanden bereits vor mehr als 3000 Jahren Fußballspiele statt. Auch wird stark vermutet, daß es bei den frühen keltischen Nationen Europas und bei den Wikingern ziemlich rauhen zeremoniellen Fußball gab. Im alten Süd- und Mittelamerika pflegte man ein Spiel namens „Tlatchi".

Die Griechen und Römer der Antike nutzten Fußballspiele zur Vorbereitung ihrer Krieger auf den Kampf. Mit den römischen Armeen breiteten sich in ganz Europa Spiele wie „Harpestum" oder „Paganica" aus, zu denen Elemente des Kickens oder Laufens mit dem Ball gehörten. Hier finden wir die europäischen Wurzeln dessen, was dann im 19. Jahrhundert zum Fußball werden sollte und es bis heute geblieben ist.

"Tsu chu" – Ceremonial Football played in China 2000 years ago.

«Tsu chu» - football rituel pratiqué en Chine il y a 2000 ans.

"Tsu chu" – Fútbol ceremonial jugado en China hace 2000 años.

„Tsu chu". – Zeremonielles Fußballspiel in China vor 2000 Jahren.

Chinese characters meaning "Football".
J. R. Witty, once an English FA official
and a keen historian, described the
symbols illustrated here as, first, "To
kick with the foot" and, second, "A ball
made with leather and filled with some-
thing to allow it to be kicked around for
recreation if you have time for it".

Caractères chinois signifiant «Football».

Signos chinos que significan "Fútbol".

Der Begriff „Fußball" in chinesischen
Schriftzeichen.

"Kemari" – Japanese ceremonial Football game derived from ancient Chinese Football. 19th Century watercolour on silk.

«Kemari» - football rituel dérivé de l'ancien football chinois. Peinture sur soie.

"Kemari" - Ceremonial juego de fútbol japonés que se deriva del antiguo fútbol chino. Siglo XIX, acuarela sobre seda.

„Kemari", ein japanisches zeremonielles Fußballspiel, entstanden nach dem alten chinesischen Vorbild. Wasserfarbe auf Seide, 19. Jahrhundert.

"Life at the Chiyoda Palace". Samurai warriors watch Kemari ceremony. Japanese woodcut in three sections by Fukuta Hatsujiki, 1897.

«La vie au palais de Chiyoda». Guerriers samourai observant une cérémonie Kerami. Gravure japonaise par Fukuta Hatsujiki, 1897.

"Vida en el palacio de Chiyoda". Guerreros Samurais mirando la ceremonia Kemai. Grabado japonés en madera en tres secciones de Fukuta Hatsujiki, 1897.

„Leben am Chiyoda-Palast". Samurai-Krieger beobachten eine Kemari-Zeremonie. Dreiteiliger Holzschnitt von Fukuta Hatsujiki, 1897.

Ancient Greek or Etruscan Ball Player.
18th Century copperplate engraving
with bistre hand colouring.

Joueur de balle étrusque ou grec. Cuivre
repoussé du 18ème siècle, avec dessin
au bistre.

Antiguo futbolista griego o etrusco.
Grabado coloreado a mano del siglo
XVIII.

Antiker griechischer oder etruskischer
Ballspieler. Handkolorierter Kupferstich, 18. Jahrhundert.

Veduta del Campo de Giesuiti à Venetia.   N. 63.   Prospect des Blaß bey den Jesuitern in Venedig.
Martin Engelbrecht excud. A. V.

Playball at Venice. Illustration from
Antonio da Salo's book "Treatise on
Games with the ball", 1555.

Jeu de balle à Venise. Illustration extraite du livre d'Antonio da Salo, «Traité sur
les jeux de balle», 1555.

Juego de pelota en Venecia. Ilustración
del libro de Antonio da Salo "Tratado
sobre los juegos de pelota", 1555.

Ballspiel in Venedig. Aus dem Buch
„Traktat über Spiele mit dem Ball" von
Antonio da Salo, 1555.

Ludus quem Itali appellant il Calcio

"Il Calcio" at Padova. Engraving by Petro Bertelli, ca. 1595.

«Il Calcio» à Padova. Gravure de Petro Bertelli, circa 1595.

"Il Calcio" en Padua. Grabado de Petro Bertelli, hacia 1595.

„Il Calcio" in Padua. Kupferstich von Petro Bertelli, ca. 1595.

Game of Pallone in a medieval German Town. Engraving by Matthäus Merian the Older, 1630.

Jeu du Pallone dans une cité médiévale germanique. Gravure de Matthäus Merian le Vieux, 1630.

Juego de Pallone en una ciudad medieval alemana. Grabado de Matthäus Merian el Viejo, 1630.

Pallone-Spiel in einer mittelalterlichen deutschen Stadt. Kupferstich von Matthäus Merian d. Ä., 1630.

Football and Handball Games in Greenland. Engraving from a travel book by Hans P. Engede, Copenhagen 1763.

Jeux de football et de handball au Groenland. Gravure extraite du recueil de voyage de Hans P. Engede, Copenhague 1763.

Juegos de fútbol y balonmano en Groenlandia. Grabado de un libro de viajes de Hans P. Engede, Copenhague, 1763.

Fußball- und Handballspiel in Grönland. Kupferstich aus einem Reisebuch von Hans P. Engede, Kopenhagen 1763.

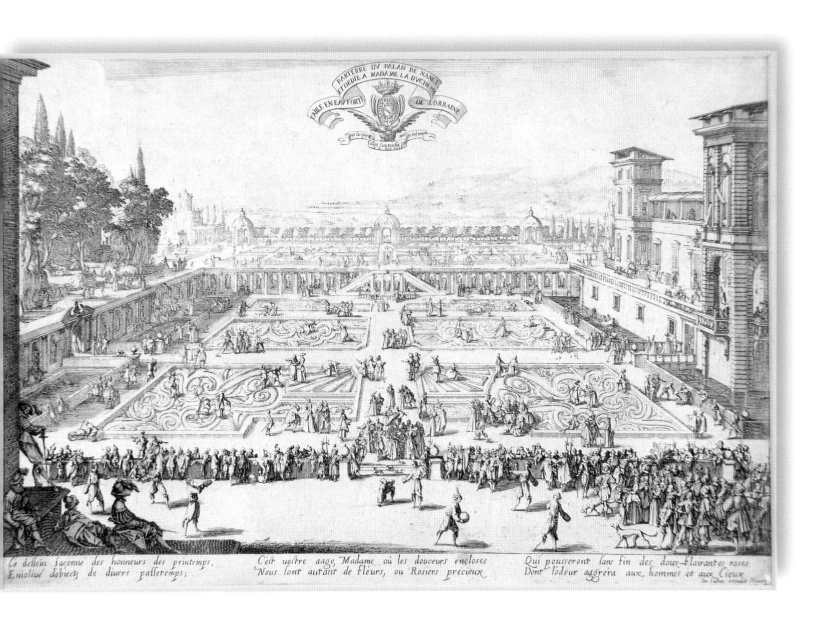

Ball Game at the Palace of Nancy, France. Engraving by Jacques Callot, 1625.

Jeux de ball sur le Palace de Nancy. Gravure de Jacques Callot, 1625.

Juego de pelota en el palacio de Nancy. Grabado de Jacques Callot, 1625.

Ballspiel am Palast von Nancy. Kupferstich von Jacques Callot, 1625.

"Ballspiel". Football in a Russian market town in winter 1810. Etching after Christian Gottfried Heinrich Geissler.

«Ballspiel». Football dans une ville russe durant l'hiver 1810. Reproduction d'aprés Christian Gottfried Heinrich Geissler.

"Ballspiel". Fútbol en una ciudad mercantil rusa en invierno de 1810. Aguafuerte según Christian Gottfried Heinrich Geissler.

„Ballspiel". Fußball in einer russischen Marktstadt, Winter 1810. Radierung nach Christian Gottfried Heinrich Geissler.

"La Soule" – This ferocious version of football was played in Normandy and Brittany. Steel engraving of 1835.

«La Soule» - Cette version très violente de football était surtout pratiquée en Normandie et en Bretagne. Gravure sur acier de 1835.

"La Soule" - Se jugaba a esta versión violenta de fútbol en Normandía y Gran Bretaña. Grabado en acero de 1835.

„La Soule". Diese rauhe Art von Fußball spielte man in der Normandie und in der Bretagne. Stahlstich, 1835.

2 Traditional European Football
Football traditionnel européen
Fútbol tradicional europeo
Traditioneller europäischer Fußball

Traditional Football games played throughout Europe in centuries past are still being staged in modern times, especially in the British Isles. They usually include an element of mob battles and chases over countryside and through water. Undertones of ancient Celtic pagan ceremonies as well as the influence of old Roman Empire army "games" can be recognized. In later years Football play was often linked to rural wedding-day celebrations in Western Europe.

Playballs used in traditional games come in many different materials, colours and sizes. Rather than being light and inflated, they are usually stuffed with hair or rags and are heavy. This indicates the rough nature of the combat, using hands and feet, with no quarter asked or given.

Les diverses formes de football traditionnelles pratiquées en Europe au cours des siècles passés, existent toujours, notamment dans les îles britanniques. Elles incluent généralement des éléments de batailles populaires et de courses à travers la campagne et les cours d'eau. On peut y déceler la trace d'anciennes cérémonies celtiques païennes et l'influence des jeux militaires de la Rome Antique. Plus tard, le football fut souvent associé à des mariages ruraux en Europe de l'Ouest.

Les ballons utilisés lors de ces parties pouvaient être faits de matériaux, de couleurs et de tailles différentes. Au lieu d'être légers et remplis d'air, ils étaient en général bourrés de cheveux ou de tissus, et étaient lourds. Ceci nous donne quelques indications quant à la rude nature du combat, où l'on utilisait les mains comme les pieds, et où l'on ne se faisait pas de quartier.

Los juegos de balompié tradicionales practicados en Europa en siglos pasados, todavía tienen lugar ahora, sobre todo en las Islas Británicas. Éstos usualmente incluyen elementos de las peleas del populacho y de persecución a través de los campos y del agua. Huellas de las antiguas ceremonias paganas celtas así como también influencias del "juegos militares" del ejercito del antiguo Imperio Romano pueden ser reconocidas. Posteriormente, el juego de balompié muchas veces tuvo relación con ceremonias de matrimonio rurales en Europa Occidental. Las pelotas utilizadas en los juegos del pasado fueron hechas de muy diferentes materiales, colores y tamaños. En vez de ser livianas e infladas, las pelotas normalmente eran rellenadas con pelos o trapos y eran pesadas, lo cual nos da indicios de lo áspero que era el combate, en que se utilizaba manos y pies, y en el cual nunca entraba tinero.

Europäische Spielarten vergangener Jahrhunderte werden heute immer noch gepflegt, vor allem auf den britischen Inseln. Gewöhnlich finden sich hier Elemente von Gruppenkampf und Verfolgungsjagden zu Land und durch Gewässer. Auch Anklänge der alten keltischen heidnischen Zeremonien sowie der Spiele in den Armeen des römischen Weltreichs sind zu beobachten. In späteren Jahren gehörte das Fußballspiel in Westeuropa oft zu den ländlichen Hochzeitszeremonien.

Man benutzte Bälle aus unterschiedlichem Material, in vielen Farben und Größen. Sie waren weder aufgeblasen noch leicht, sondern noch ausgestopft mit Tierhaar oder Lumpen und ziemlich schwer. Dies weist zugleich auf die noch rauhe Natur des Kampfspiels hin, das mit Händen und Füßen betrieben wurde und bei dem niemandem in den Sinn kam, dafür etwa Geld zu fordern oder zu zahlen.

Oliver Cromwell, the 17th Century Lord Protector of Great Britain, played Football at Cambridge University in the early 1600s.

Oliver Cromwell, Lord chancelleir de Grande Bretagne au 17ème siècle, jouait au football à l'université de Cambridge au début des années 1600.

Oliver Cromwell, el Lord Protector de Gran Bretaña jugaba al fútbol en la universidad de Cambridge a principios del siglo XVII.

Oliver Cromwell, späterer Lordprotektor von Großbritannien, spielte in seiner Universitätszeit in Cambridge zu Beginn des 17. Jahrhunderts Fußball.

Football in the streets of London. Etching by H. Heath, ca. 1820.

Football dans les rues de Londres. Gravure de H. Heath, circa 1820.

Fútbol en las calles de Londres. Aguafuerte de H. Heath, hacia 1820.

Fußball in den Straßen von London. Radierung von H. Heath, ca. 1820.

Foot Ball. Engraving by George Hunt after Robert Cruikshank, 1820.

Foot Ball. Gravure de George Hunt d´après Robert Cruikshank, 1820.

Fútbol. Grabado de George Hunt, copia según Robert Cruikshank, 1820.

Foot Ball. Kupferstich von George Hunt nach Robert Cruishank, 1820.

Scottish clans at play. Etching after the Russian artist Stephanoff, 1815.

Clans écossais en train de jouer. Gravure d´après l´artiste russe Stephanoff, 1815.

Clanes escoceses jugando. Aguafuerte del artista ruso Stephanoff, 1815.

Schottische Clans beim Spiel. Radierung nach dem russischen Maler Stephanoff, 1815.

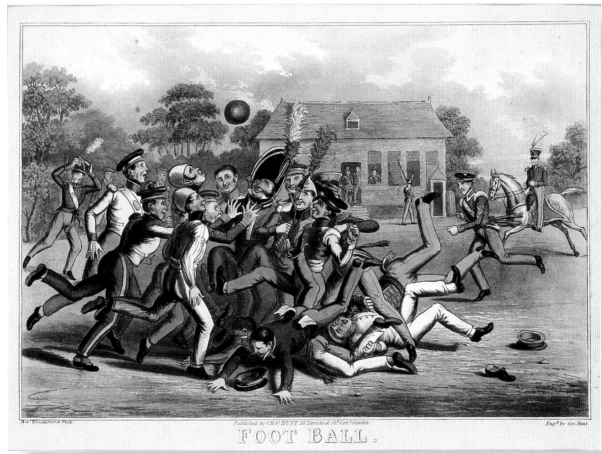

Apprentice Football. A pastiche of 17th century London city life by Amedee Forestier, painted in the early 20th century.

Joueur apprenant le football. Pastiche de Amedee Forestier peint au début du 20ème siècle et représentant la vie dans la City de Londres des années 1700.

Futból para principiantes. Imagen de la vida ciudadana de Londres de Amedee Forestier, pintada a principios del siglo XX.

Anfänger-Fußball. Sittenbild aus dem London des 17. Jahrhunderts von Amedee Forestier, gemalt zu Beginn unseres Jahrhunderts.

Foot-Ball. "The Rosh". Royal Military Academy cadets play near London. Hand-coloured lithograph by W. H. Pearson, 1857.

Foot-Ball. «Le Rosh». Les cadets de l'Académie royale jouant près de Londres. Lithographie à la main de W. H. Pearson, 1857.

Foot-Ball. "The Rosh". Cadetes de la Academia Real juegan cerca de Londres. Litografía coloreada a mano de W. H. Pearson, 1857.

Foot-Ball. „The Rosh". Kadetten der Königlichen Militärakademie beim Spiel nahe London. Handkolorierte Lithographie von W. H. Pearson, 1857.

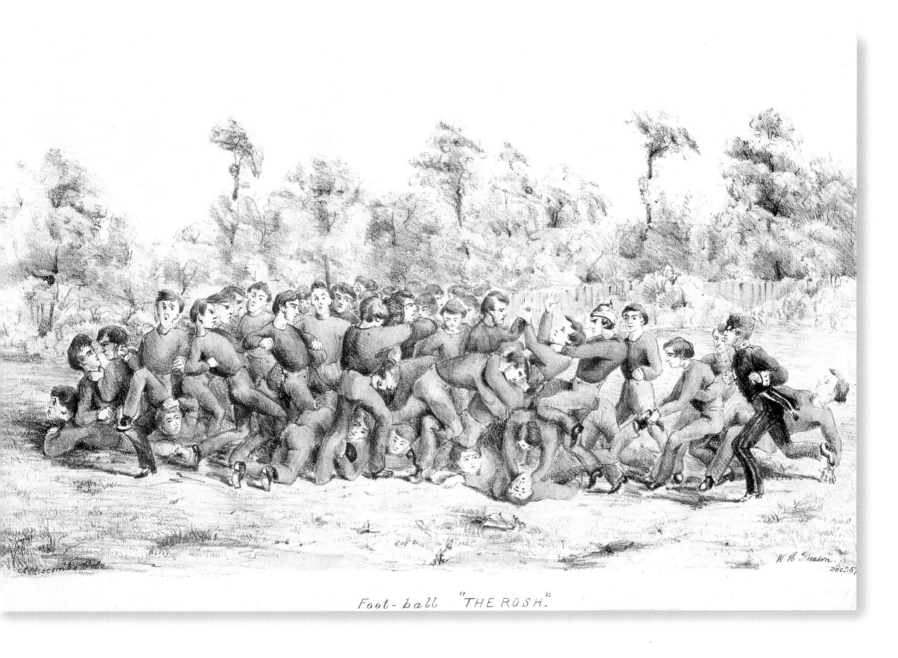

Foot-ball "THE ROSH".

Football at Kingston, 1846. The contest to win a gold-painted ball was subsequently banned for its violence. Woodcut by Phillipson of Kingston, 1846.

Football à Kingston, 1846. La compétition pour gagner une balle recouverte d'or fut par la suite interdite à cause de son extrême violence. Gravure de Phillipson de Kingston, 1846.

Fútbol en Kingston, 1846. La competición para ganar un balón pintado de oro fue prohibida más tarde por su violencia. Grabado en madera de Phillipson of Kingston, 1846.

Football in Kingston, 1846. Der Wettbewerb um einen goldbemalten Ball wurde kurz darauf wegen seiner Brutalität verboten. Holzschnitt von Phillipson of Kingston, 1846.

FOOT BALL, KINGSTON-UPON-THAMES,
SHROVE TUESDAY, FEB. 24TH, 1846.

Camp-Ball. Village boys and shepherds play an ancient form of cross-country European Football Primitive oil-painting, mid-19th century.

Camp-Ball. Garçons de village et bergers pratiquant une forme ancienne de football européen à base de courses dans la campagne. Peinture à l´huile du milieu du 19ème siècle.

Camp-Ball. Chicos y pastores juegan una forma antigua de „Cross-country" fútbol europeo. Pintura primitiva, oleo sobre tela, mediados del siglo XIX.

Camp-Ball. Dorfjungen und Schäfer bei einer alten Form europäischen Gelände-Fußballs. Naives Gemälde, Mitte 19. Jahrhundert.

Football. Painting by Thomas Webster RA, 1839. The most famous Football image of the 19th century. Exhibited at the Royal Academy, London. Oils on board.

Football. Peinture de Thomas Webster RA, 1839. Illustration du football la plus célèbre du 19ème siècle, exposée à la Royal Académie de Londres.

Football. Cuadro de Thomas Webster RA, 1839. La imagen más famosa del siglo XIX, exhibida en la Royal Academy de Londres.

Football. Ölgemälde von Thomas Webster RA, 1839. Die berühmteste Fußballdarstellung des 19. Jahrhunderts, ausgestellt in der Londoner Royal Academy.

Traditional footballs, some still in use.

Kirkwall ball from the Orkney islands off the Scottish coast, painted in two colours to flash in the air.

Footballs traditionnelles encore pratiqué.

Kirkwall ball des îles Orkney sur la côte écossaise peinte de deux couleurs pour être plus visible lorsqu´elle est en l´air.

Balones tradicionales, todavía en uso.

Balón de Kirkwall de las islas de Orkney cerca de la costa escocesa, pintado en dos colores para resplandecer en el aire.

Traditionelle Fußbälle, einige davon noch heute in Gebrauch.

Ball aus Kirkwall, auf den Orkney-Inseln vor der schottischen Küste, zweifarbig bemalt, um in der Luft entsprechend zu glänzen.

Workington ball , a very solid leather ball, thrown as well as kicked; a Northern England game

Workington ball, balle très dure en cuir, aussi bien lancée que frappée; jeu du Nord de l´Angleterre.

Balón Workington, un balón muy sólido de cuero lanzado a mano y a pie, un juego del norte de Inglaterra.

Ball aus Workington in Nordengland. Ein solider Lederball, der sowohl geworfen als auch gekickt wurde.

Ashbourne ball. The Ashbourne games in Derby, in the middle of England, are famous for the huge painted leather ball and for the phrase "a local Derby match" – a title given for over a century to those matches played between close rivals.

Ashbourne ball. Les parties d´Ashbourne à Derby, au centre de l´Angleterre, sont célèbres pour leur énorme ballons en cuir peint, et pour l´expression «un Derby local», titre donné depuis près d´un siècle à tout match disputé entre équipes voisines.

Balón de Ashbourne. Los partidos de Ashbourne en Derby en el centro de Inglaterra son famosos por el enorme balón de cuero pintado y por la frase "un partido local de Derby" - un título dado durante más de un siglo a aquellos partidos jugados por dos rivales íntimos.

Ashbourne-Ball aus Derby in Mittelengland. Die dortigen Ashbourne-Spiele sind berühmt wegen ihres großen bemalten Lederballs und wegen der Bezeichnung „ein lokales Derby-Match" – die seit mehr als 100 Jahren für Spiele zwischen Lokalrivalen (Ortsderby) benutzt wird.

Leather bottle "ball". Old leather bottles, their shape reminiscent of footballs, frequently finished their lives kicked about village greens.

Bouteille de cuir e forme de balle. Ces vieilles bouteilles finissaient en général sur le terrain du village, leur forme rappelant celle d'un ballon.

Balón de tipo "botella de cuero". Viejas botellas de cuero cuya forma recuerda a balones terminaron con frecuencia su vida siendo lanzados en los prados de los pueblos.

Lederflaschen-„Ball". Alte Leder-flaschen, in der Form an Fußbälle erin-nernd, beendeten ihr Leben häufig, indem sie über den Dorfanger gekickt wurden.

Harrow School Ball. The ball used in games of "Footer" unique to Harrow School in North London is a huge, glasped-hands construction said to resemble Footballs used in medieval times.

Ballon de l'école d'Harrow. La balle était utilisée lors des partie de «footer» propres à l'école d'Harrow au nord de Londres. Il s'agissait d'un ballon énorme fait à la main, dont on dit qu'il ressemblait à ceux utilisés au Moyen Age.

Balón "Harrow School". El balón usado en partidos de "Footer" únicamente en Harrow School en el norte de Londres, es una construcción enorme encajada que debe asemejarse a los balones usados en los tiempos medievales.

Harrow School-Ball. Der allein beim „Footer"-Spiel an der Schule im Norden Londons benutzte Ball ist ein besonders großes Exemplar, von dem es heißt, es erinnere an mittelalterliche Fußbälle.

3 Football Revolution – The Birth of a Game
La révolution du football – Naissance d'un jeu
Revolución del fútbol – El nacimiento de un juego
Revolutionierung des Fußballs – Die Geburt eines Spiels

"Association Football", "Soccer", or, nowadays, "Football" was invented in England in the 1860s and 1870s. "Football" was, and strictly speaking still is, the generic term for all games where kicking the ball is part of the rules. It is important to understand that "Football" began to be used specifically to describe Association Football in Europe some time after the Football Association was formed in London in 1863. The Football Association was not set up with the intention of creating a "new" game. The wealthy young Britons who formed the Association had all attended exclusive schools, each fanatically proud of their own traditions and each with their own Football rules. Now, the Football Association – with their universally acceptable rules for one game only – came into being to provide a game overseen by gentlemen for young gentlemen. It was some years before the world game of today became faintly recognizable.

Le «Association Football», le «Soccer», aujourd'hui le football, fut fondée en Angleterre durant les années 1860 et 1870. Au sens stricte du terme, le «Football» était, et est encore le terme générique donné à tout jeux dans lequel tirer dans une balle fait partie des règles. Il est important de comprendre que le mot «Football» ne désigna spécifiquement l'Association du Football en Europe que quelques temps après sa création à Londres en 1863. L'Association du Football ne fut pas créée afin d'instaurer un nouveau jeu. Les jeunes sportifs anglais qui faisaient partie de l'Association, étaient tous issus d'écoles privées, fiers jusqu'au fanatisme de leurs traditions et de leurs propres règlements. L'Association du Football, aux règles universellement acceptées pour un jeu uniformisé, donna naissance à un jeu contrôlé par des gentlemens et réservé aux jeunes hommes de bonne famille. C'était quelques années avant que le jeu mondial d'aujourd'hui, ne commence à être reconnu.

El "Association Football", el "Soccer" – hoy nuestro fútbol – fue una invención en la Inglaterra de los años 1860 y 1870. El "Football" era y es todavía, el término genérico para todos los juegos en que el patear la pelota es una parte de las reglas. Es importante entender que el termino "Fútbol" se empezó a usar específicamente para describir al "Association Football" en Europa, algún tiempo después de que se hubo formado la Asociación de Fútbol en Londres en 1863.
La Federación de Fútbol no se fundó con el propósito de crear un "nuevo" juego. Los jóvenes ricos ingleses que formaron la Asociación eran estudiantes de colegios exclusivos, donde cada grupo era fanáticamente orgulloso de su propias tradiciones y tenía sus propias reglas de fútbol.
La Federación, con sus reglas universalmente aceptadas para un solo juego, surgió para poner a disposición un juego controlado por caballeros para jóvenes caballeros. Y así, el juego mundial de hoy día poco a poco se desarrolló.

„Association Football", „Soccer" – heute unser Fußball – wurde im England der sechziger und siebziger Jahre des 19. Jahrhunderts entwickelt. „Football" war dabei der Oberbegriff für alle Spiele, bei denen das Kicken des Balls zu den Regeln gehörte – was sich bis heute nicht geändert hat. Dabei ist wichtig zu wissen, daß man den Begriff „Football" einige Zeit nach Gründung der Football Association in London 1863 speziell für den „Association Football" in Europa zu benutzen begann.
Die Gründung der Football Association erfolgte nicht mit der Absicht, ein „neues" Spiel zu kreieren. Die wohlhabenden jungen Briten, welche die Association bildeten, hatten allesamt exklusive Schulen besucht, jede einzelne stolz auf ihre Tradition, und jede mit eigenen Fußball-Regeln. Mit ihren überall anwendbaren Regeln für nur noch eine Spielart präsentierte die Football Association nunmehr ein Spiel für junge Gentlemen, kontrolliert von Gentlemen. Nur wenige Jahre später sollte sich der heute weltweit gepflegte Fußball mehr und mehr durchsetzen.

"Footer" at Harrow School, with esoteric rules and the giant ball. Etching from a drawing by Walter Cox, 1887.

«Footer» à l´école d´Harrow aux règles ésotériques et à l´énorme ballon. Reproduction d´après un dessin de Walter Cox, 1887.

"Footer" en Harrow School con reglas esotéricas y el balón gigante. Aguafuerte según un dibujo de Walter Cox, 1887.

„Footer" an der Harrow School, mit nur hier geltenden Regeln und dem riesigen Ball. Radierung nach einer Zeichnung von Walter Cox, 1887.

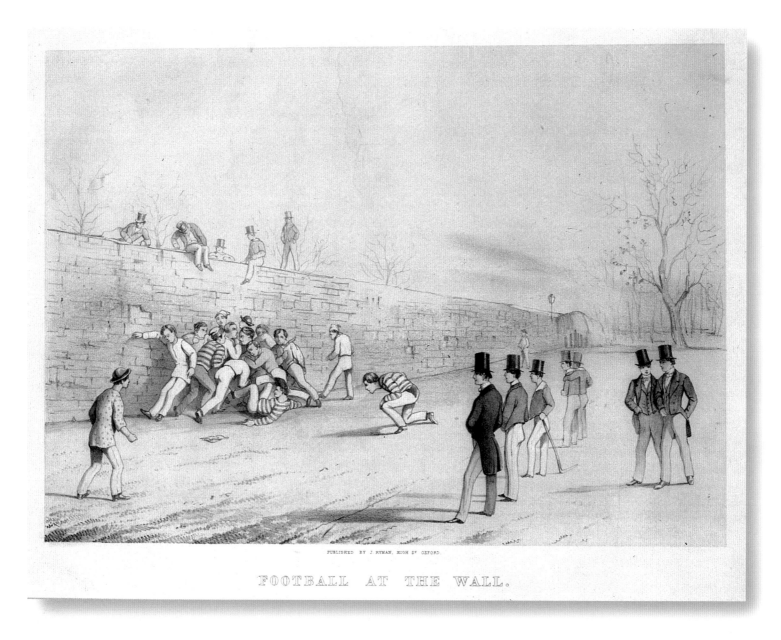

FOOTBALL AT THE WALL.

"Football at the wall", another old school game played at Eton. Mid-19th century lithograph.

«Le football au mur», un autre vieux jeu issu d´une école et pratiqué à Eton. Lithogaphie du milieu du 19ème siècle.

"Fútbol contra el muro", otro antiguo juego de escuela jugado en Eton. Litografía de mediados del siglo XIX.

"Football gegen die Mauer". Ein weiteres altes Schul-Spiel, gepflegt in Eton. Lithographie, Mitte 19. Jahrhundert.

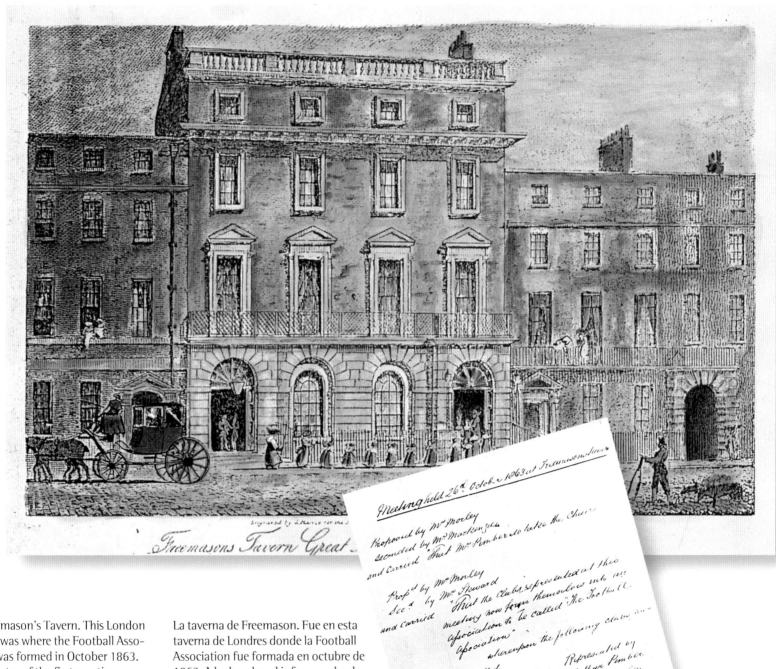

The Freemason's Tavern. This London hostelry was where the Football Association was formed in October 1863. The minutes of the first meeting are reproduced.

La taverna de Freemason. Fue en esta taverna de Londres donde la Football Association fue formada en octubre de 1863. A la derecha, el informe sobre la primera reunión de la FA.

La taverne Freemason. Ce fut dans cette auberge londonïènne que fut fondée l'Association du Football en octobre 1863. A droite, le court rapport de la première session.

Freemason's Tavern. In diesem Londoner Gasthaus wurde im Oktober 1863 die Football Association gegründet. Rechts die knappe Notiz von der ersten Sitzung.

A 19th century caricature of Lord Kinnaird, the first president of the Football Association.

Caricature du 19ème siècle de Lord Kinnaird, premier président de l'Association du Football.

Una caricatura del siglo XIX de Lord Kinnaird, el primer presidente de la Football Association.

Lord Kinnaird, der erste Präsident der Football Association. Karikatur, 19. Jahrhundert.

England vs. Scotland 1872 – the first official Soccer international. Woodcut from drawings by W. Ralston (left) and an early photograph of the Scottish team in 1896 in 1896 (above).

Angleterre – Ecosse, première rencontre internationale officielle de Soccer. Gravures d´un dessin de W. Ralston (à gauche) et l´une des première photographie de l'équipe écossaise, 1896 (en haut).

Inglaterra contra Escocia 1872 – el primer partido oficial de fútbol internacional. Grabado en madera según dibujos de W. Ralston (a la izquierda) y una foto antigua del equipo escocés 1896 (arriba).

England – Schottland 1872, das erste Fußball-Länderspiel. Holzschnitt nach Zeichnungen von W. Ralston (links) sowie eine frühe Photographie des schottischen Teams von 1896 (oben).

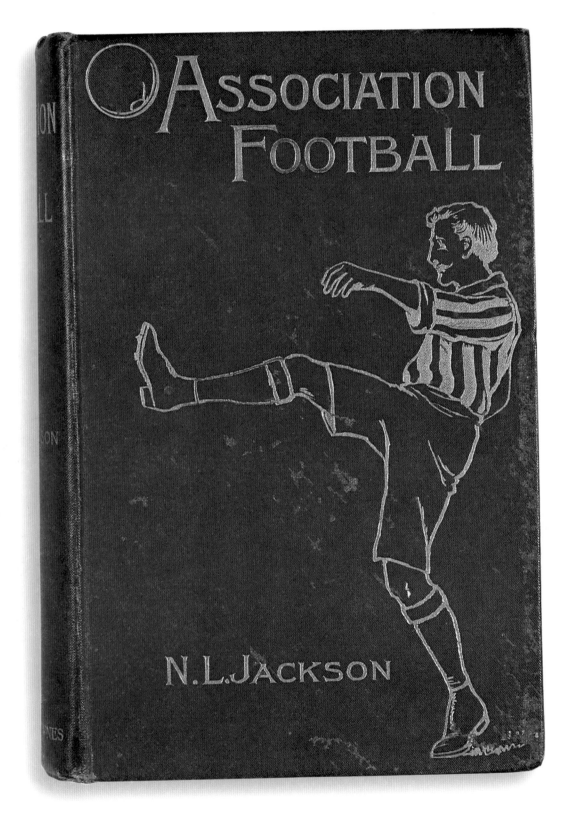

This book was published in 1899, one of the first in what was become a multitude of books of the game.

Ce livre fut publié en 1899 comme un des premiers dans l'abondance de littérature de football.

Este libro fue publicado en 1899 como uno de los primeros en la gran variedad de literatura sobre el fútbol.

Dieses Buch erschien 1899 als eines der ersten in der Fülle von Fußball-Literatur.

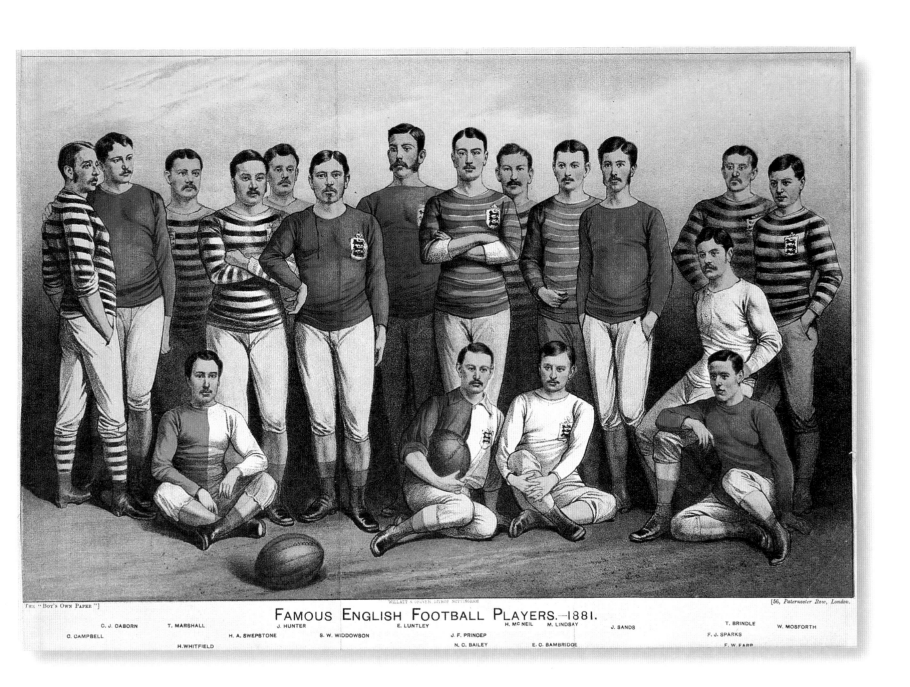

FAMOUS ENGLISH FOOTBALL PLAYERS.—1881.

THE "BOY'S OWN PAPER."] WILLATT & SPENCER LITHOS NOTTINGHAM [56, *Paternoster Row*, London.

C. J. CABORN   T. MARSHALL   J. HUNTER   E. LUNTLEY   H. McNEIL   M. LINDSAY   J. SANDS   T. BRINDLE   W. MOSFORTH

C. CAMPBELL   H. A. SWEPSTONE   S. W. WIDDOWSON   J. F. PRINCEP   N. C. BAILEY   E. C. BAMBRIDGE   F. J. SPARKS

H. WHITFIELD   F. W. FARR

Famous English Footballers, 1881. Coloured Lithograph. Such a grouping, of Soccer players and Rugby Union players together, was perfectly acceptable in 1881. A short time later the barrier between the Association and the Union made such a picture impossible.

Footballeurs anglais célèbres, 1881. Litographie en couleur. Un tel rassemblement de joueurs de Soccer et de l'Union du Rugby était tout à fait imaginable en 1881. Peu de temps après, la séparation entre l'Association et l'Union rendit impossible de telles photos.

Futbolistas famosos ingleses, 1881. Litografía coloreada. Tal agrupación de futbolistas y jugadores de la Rugby Union juntos era absolutamente aceptable en 1881. Poco tiempo después la ruptura entre la Asociación y la Rugby Union hicieron imposibles tales imágenes.

Berühmte britische Fußballer, Farblithographie 1881. Zu dieser Zeit war die gemeinsame Abbildung von Fußball- und Rugbyspielern noch möglich. Kurz darauf erfolgte dann der Bruch zwischen Football Association und Rugby Union.

4 The Giant Awakes
L'émergence d'un géant
El despertar del gigante
Der Gigant erwacht

From 1863 to 1872, Association Football was scarcely a success. Teams often ignored the new rules. Most serious clubs were for gentlemen only. It was the introduction of the FA Cup and international matches that saved the game from ignominy, although for many years, up to the mid 1890s, Rugby Union became the premier code, drawing vast crowds for the era in the North of England.

With the surge of interest created by cup competition, "the new game" was also transformed by the advent of inexpensive, mass-produced equipment.

Smooth, round balls, lighter despite their thick skin of leather, demanded flat pitches and better playing technique. Quite rapidly there evolved a game radically different from any Football played anywhere previously. And thus flowered the magnetic spectacle still recognisable over 100 years later.

De 1863 à 1872, l'Association du Football ne remporta qu'un succès très mitigé. Le plus souvent, les équipes ignoraient les nouvelles règles. Les clubs les plus sérieux n'étaient réservés qu'aux hommes provenant d'une certaine société. Ce fut l'introduction de la coupe de l'Association du Football et des matchs internationaux qui permirent au jeu de sortir de l'anonymat, bien que jusqu'au milieu des années 1890, l'Union du Rugby, qui mobilisait de vastes foules au nord de l'Angleterre, demeura la référence.

Le «nouveau jeu» fut conjointement transformé par l'apparition d'un intérêt créé par la Coupe, et l'arrivée d'un équipement populaire bon marché.

Des ballons ronds, doux et plus légers malgré leur revêtement de cuir épais, exigeaient un contrôle plus subtile de la balle, ainsi qu'une meilleure technique de jeu. Ce jeu évolua dès lors très rapidement vers un football radicalement différent de celui pratiqué auparavant. De cette évolution naquît le spectacle magique et «accrocheur» reconnaissable plus de cent ans plus tard.

De 1863 a 1872, el "Association Football" apenas tuvo éxito. Los equipos a menudo ignoraban las nuevas reglas. La mayoría de los clubs serios era solamente para caballeros. Recién la introducción de la Copa FA y de partidos internacionales dio reconocimiento al juego, aunque por muchos años, hasta alrededor de 1895, la Federación de Rugby tenía mayor importancia, ya que atraía a grandes masas en el Norte de Inglaterra.

Con el interés surgido por la creación del campeonato por la Copa, el "nuevo juego" se transformó al comenzar la producción en masa de artículos deportivos de precio moderado. Redondas, suaves pelotas, más ligeras a pesar de su gruesa piel de cuero, exigían el juego raso y una mejor técnica de juego. Rápidamente se desarrolló un juego totalmente diferente de cualquier fútbol jugado con anterioridad en cualquier sitio. Así floreció este magnético espectáculo, todavía reconocible después de más de 100 años.

Von 1863 bis 1872 war dem Association Football zunächst wenig Erfolg beschieden. Oft ignorierten die Teams die neuen Regeln. In die meisten seriösen Klubs nahm man nur „Gentlemen" auf. Erst die Einführung des FA Cups sowie internationaler Matchs brachte dem Spiel allgemeine Anerkennung, obwohl bis etwa 1895 die Rugby Union noch an erster Stelle stand und ihre Spiele, vor allem in Nordengland, große Zuschauermengen anzogen.

Mit dem durch die Einführung des Cup-Wettbewerbs steigenden Interesse erfuhr das „neue Spiel" weitere Veränderung – nun begann die Massenproduktion von neuartiger und für jedermann erschwinglicher Spielausrüstung. Die neuen weichen und runden Bälle, trotz ihrer dicken Lederhülle leichter, erforderten das flache Spiel und eine bessere Technik. Sehr rasch entstand damit ein Spiel, das sich radikal von allem bisher gepflegten Football unterschied. Und so erblühte jenes magnetische Spektakel, das noch 100 Jahre später nichts von seinem Reiz eingebüßt hat.

West Bromwich Albion vs. Renton, 1888. "The First World Club Championship". Woodcut from a London magazine.

West Bromwich Albion – Renton, 1888. «La première club coupe du monde». Gravure du London magazine.

West Bromwich Albion contra Renton, 1888. "El primer club campeonato mundial". Grabado en madera de una revista de Londres.

West Bromwich Albion – Renton, 1888. „Die erste Klubmeisterschaft der Welt". Holzschnitt aus einem Londoner Magazin.

Renton F. C., 1888/89.
"The World Champions".

Renton F. C., 1888/89.
«Les champions du monde».

Renton F. C., 1888/89.
"Los campeones mundiales".

Renton F. C., 1888/89.
„Die Weltmeister".

Oxford vs. Cambridge. Hand-coloured print, c1895.

Oxford – Cambridge. Gravure colorée à la main, vers 1895.

Oxford contra Cambridge. Litografía coloreada a mano, hacia 1895.

Oxford – Cambridge. Handkolorierter Druck, um 1895.

The Corinthians. This legendary amateur club was formed in 1882 by "Pa" Jackson (top left) and was the "England" team through which many European and South American countries were introduced to high-minded ideals of sportsmanship.

Les Corinthians. Ce club d'amateurs légendaire fut fondé en 1882 par «Pa» Jackson, en haut à gauche, et l'équipe d'Angleterre qui fit découvrir à nombreux pays européens et sud-américaines l'idéal du sport d'équipe.

Los Corintios. El legendario Club de aficionados fue fundado en 1882 por "Pa" Jackson (arriba a la izquierda) y fue el equipo "Inglaterra" por el cual muchos paises europeos y suramericanos fueron introducidos en los altos ideales del deporte.

The Corinthians. Der legendäre Amateurklub wurde 1882 von „Pa" Jackson (oben links) gegründet und bildete wenig später jenes „England"-Team, das in vielen Ländern Europas und Südamerikas die hohen Ideale des neuen Sports präsentierte.

Legendary players of the 19th century

Footballeurs légendaires du 19ème siècle.

Futbolistas legendarios del siglo XIX.

Legendäre Fußballer des 19. Jahrhunderts

Ralph. T. Squire

Ralph T. Squire from Old Westminster's F. C.

Ralph T. Squire du club Old Westminster.

Ralph T. Squire del Old Westminster´s F. C.

Ralph T. Squire von Old Westminster's F. C.

G. O. Smith, the Corinthian and England centre-forward

G. O. Smith, avant centre de l´équipe d´Angleterre et des Corinthians.

G. O. Smith, el delantero de los Corintios y del equipo inglés.

G. O. Smith, Mittelstürmer bei den Corinthians und im England-Team.

C. B. Fry, another legendary Corinthian figure and world record holder for the long-jump.

C. B. Fry, autre figure légendaire des Corinthians et détenteur du record du monde en saut en longueur.

C. B. Fry, otra figura legendaria corintia y poseedor de la marca de salto de longitud.

C. B. Fry, ein weiterer berühmter Spieler der Corinthians, dazu Weltrekordler im Weitsprung.

This painted spelter clock set (ca. 1900) is based on the Corinthian figures of G. O. Smith (on top of the clock) and C. B. Fry (one of the other two figures). Whilst wealthy amateurs were playing the game, expensive souvenirs with quality were produced in Britain.

Sur cette horloge peinte (circa 1900), sont représentés les joueurs des Corinthians G. O. Smith en haut, et C. B. Fry (l'une de deux autres silhouettes). Alors que des amateurs fougueux faisaient le football, des souvenirs de prix à la gloire de ces équipes, étaient produits en Angleterre.

Este juego de relojes de cinc pintado (hacia 1900) está basado en los corintios G. O. Smith (en la parte de arriba) y C. B. Fry (uno de los otros dos personajes). Ya que jugaban aficionados ricos, los partidos se producían recuerdos caros de alta calidad en Gran Bretaña.

Die Skulpturen dieser bemalten Tisch-uhr-Gruppe, ca. 1900, zeigen die Corinthians-Spieler G. O. Smith (auf der Uhr) und C. B. Fry (eine der anderen Figuren). Wohlhabende Amateure betrieben das Spiel, entsprechend kost-spielig und qualitätsvoll waren die produzierten Souvenirs.

Oxford University Association XI., 1878.
A fine team group.

Association XI de l'université d'Oxford,
1878. Une équipe de haute volée.

Asociación XI. de la Universidad de
Oxford, 1878. Un gran equipo.

Oxford University Association XI., 1878.
Eine gute Universitätsmannschaft.

The 1899 Cup Final: Derby County vs. Sheffield United. Woodcut from drawing by Ralph Cleaver.

Finale de la Coupe en 1899: le comté de Derby contre Sheffield United. Gravure d'après un dessin de Ralph Cleaver.

El final de la copa de 1899: Derby County contra Sheffield United. Grabado en madera de un dibujo de Ralph Cleaver.

Endspiel um den FA Cup 1899: Derby County – Sheffield United. Holzschnitt nach einer Zeichnung von Ralph Cleaver.

Typical Football-Woodcuts of the 1890s.

Oxford and Cambridge vs. London, 1891.

Gravure typique relative au football autour de 1890.

Oxford et Cambridge contre Londres. 1891.

Grabados típicos en madera de los años 90 del siglo pasado.

Oxford y Cambridge contra Londres, 1891.

Typische Fußball-Holzschnitte aus den Jahren nach 1890.

Oxford/Cambridge – London, 1891.

FOOTBALL.—OXFORD AND CAMBRIDGE v. LONDON.

THE FINAL FOR THE ASSOCIATION CUP AT KENNINGTON OVAL.

The Final for the Association Cup at Kennington Oval, 1891.

La finale de la Coupe de l'Association à Kennington Oval, 1891.

El final de la Copa de la Asociación en el Kennington Oval, 1891.

Endspiel um den FA Cup im Kennington Oval, 1891.

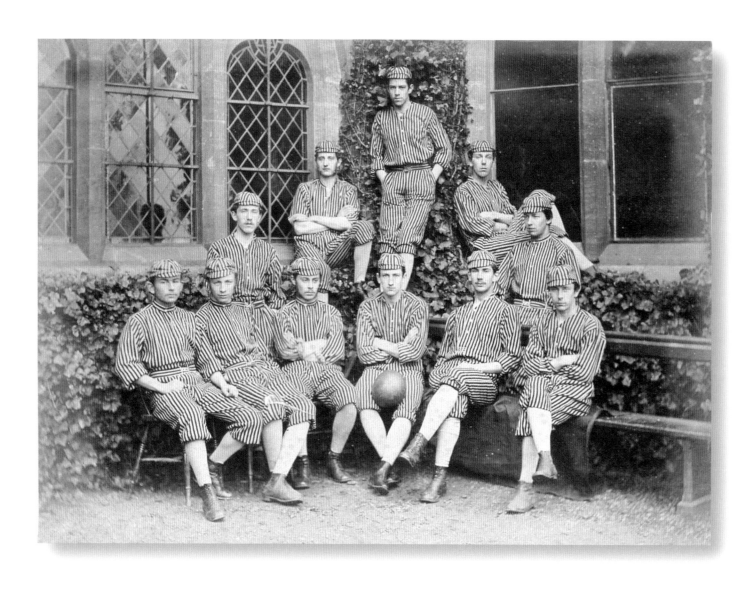

Two original photographs in sepia of Harrow Footer teams 1870 and 1871.

Deux photographies d'origine en sépia des équipes de Footer d'Harrow des années 1870 et 1871.

Dos tempranas fotos de los equipos de "Footer" de la Harrow School 1870 y 1871.

Zwei frühe Photos von „Footer"-Teams der Harrow School, 1870 und 1871.

5 The First League
La première ligue
La primera liga
Die erste Liga

The world's first league was formed in April 1888. The driving force was William McGregor, a Scottish shopkeeper, teetotal and deeply religious, chairman of the Aston Villa club in Birmingham which later became the world's first "super club". The league came just in time for Football, which was struggling to find its true role yet again after the legalization of professional teams in 1885. The forces of amateurism, then represented by the public schools and universities and their powerful position in British society, still saw paid play as an evil. However, strictly organized weekly league competition proved to be the foundation stone of the professional game. And also the foundation stone for an amazing series of printed paper cards, the so called "Baines cards" – the first brilliant commercial project to spring from popular sports with mass appeal.

La première ligue au monde fut créée en avril 1888 sur l'initiative de William Mc Gregor, un commerçant écossais radicalement opposé à toute consommation d'alcool, et profondément religieux. Il dirigeait l'Aston Villa Club de Birmingham, qui devint plus tard le premier club du monde. La Ligue arriva juste au bon moment pour le football, qui cherchait son vrai rôle depuis la légalisation des équipes professionnelles en 1885. Les partisans d'un sport d'amateur représentés par les écoles et universités très influentes au sein de la société britannique, considéraient comme malsain l'introduction du facteur argent dans le jeu.
Les compétitions hebdomadaires organisées par la Ligue furent à la base du sport professionnel et donnèrent naissance à une surprenante série de cartes imprimées appelées «Baines cards», premier projet commercial ingénieux né d'un sport populaire et tourné vers les masses.

La primera liga del mundo se formó en abril de 1888. La fuerza motora fue William McGregor, un tendero escocés, abstinente y profundamente religioso, presidente del Club Aston Villa en Birmingham, el cual después se convirtió en el primer "super club" del mundo. La liga se formó precisamente a tiempo para el fútbol, que otra vez estaba luchando por hallar su verdadero papel después de la legalización de equipos profesionales en 1885. Las fuerzas de los equipos aficionados, en aquella época representadas por los colegios públicos y las universidades y con una posición de poder en la sociedad británica, vieron con muy malos ojos el juego pagado.
Sin embargo, los campeonatos de la liga puntualmente organizados cada semana, se convirtieron en la piedra fundamental del juego profesional. Al mismo tiempo se dio inicio a una asombrosa serie de figuras impresas, las llamadas "Baines cards", primer fantástico proyecto comercial que surgió de un deporte de masas.

Im April 1888 entstand die erste Liga der Welt. Treibende Kraft dabei war William McGregor, ein zutiefst religiöser, aus Schottland stammender Ladenbesitzer und Vorsitzender des Clubs Aston Villa in Birmingham – welcher später zum ersten „Super-Club" der Welt werden sollte.
Die Liga kam für den Fußball, der nach der Legalisierung von Profiteams 1885 erneut um seine eigentliche Rolle kämpfen mußte, gerade zur rechten Zeit. Denn die Kräfte aus dem Amateurlager – damals vor allem die Public Schools und Universitäten mit ihrer einflußreichen Position in der britischen Gesellschaft – betrachteten das bezahlte Spiel immer noch als ein Übel.
Doch der straff organisierte wöchentliche Liga-Wettbewerb sollte sich als Grundstein für den Profi-Fußball erweisen. Wie auch für eine bestechende Serie gedruckter Karten, die „Baines cards" – das erste brillante kommerzielle Projekt in Verbindung mit einem populären Massensport.

William Mc Gregor, Chairman of the Aston Villa club in Birmingham, was the driving force for forming the world's first league in April 1888. Stylish portrait by the sports cartoonist "Rip".

La première Ligue au monde fut fondée en avril 1888 sous l'impulsion de William Mc Gregor, président de l'Aston Villa club à Birmingham. Portrait stylisé du dessinateur sportif «Rip».

William Mc Gregor, presidente del Aston Villa Club en Birmingham fue la fuerza motriz para formar la primera liga del mundo en abril 1888. Retrato estilizado del dibujante de deportes "Rip".

William McGregor, Präsident des Fußballklubs Aston Villa in Birmingham, war die treibende Kraft bei der Einführung der ersten Liga der Welt im April 1888. Stilisiertes Porträt von dem Sportkarikaturisten „Rip".

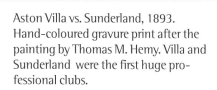

Aston Villa vs. Sunderland, 1893. Hand-coloured gravure print after the painting by Thomas M. Hemy. Villa and Sunderland were the first huge professional clubs.

Aston Villa contre Sunderland, 1893. Gravure colorée à la main. Villa et Sunderland furent les premiers grands clubs professionnels.

Aston Villa contra Sunderland, 1893. Grabado coloreado a mano según la pintura de Thomas M. Hemy. Villa y Sunderland fueron los primeros grandes clubs profesionales.

Aston Villa – Sunderland, 1893. Handkolorierte Gravüre nach dem Gemälde von Thomas M. Hemy. Villa und Sunderland waren die ersten bedeutenden Profi-Klubs.

A FOOT-BALL MATCH

England vs. Scotland, ca. 1890. Machine stitched silk picture, Scotland in their original strip of magenta and gold stripes. The giant goalkeeper is probably the Corinthian W. R. Moon.

L´Angleterre contre l´Ecosse vers 1890. Peinture sur soie représentant les Ecossais dans leurs maillots à rayures magenta et or. Le gardien de but géant est probablement le Corinthian W. R. Moon.

Inglaterra contra Escocia, hacia 1890. Dibujo bordado a máquina sobre seda, Escocia en su original franja roja y a rayas de oro. El portero gigante es probablemente el Corintio W. R. Moon.

England – Schottland, ca. 1890. Das maschinengestickte Seidenbild zeigt die Schotten in ihren goldgestreiften Jerseys. Der riesenhafte Torhüter ist wahrscheinlich der Corinthians-Spieler W. R. Moon.

England vs. Wales, 1888. Framed cap and programme. The cap is probably from Clapham Rovers, an early London club.

L'Angleterre contre Wales, 1888. Béret et programme. Le béret provient vraisemblablement d'un club londonien de la première heure, le Clapham Rovers.

Inglaterra contra Wales, 1888. Gorra y programa en un marco. La gorra es probablemente de Clapham Rovers, un antiguo club de Londres.

England – Wales, 1888. Im Rahmen eine Mütze (wahrscheinlich vom Londoner Klub Clapham Rovers) sowie das Programm zum Länderspiel.

Baines cards. These printed paper cards were the first brilliant commercial project to spring from popular sports with mass appeal. On the backs of the cards, sold in packets at small shops and collected by fans, were often advertisements.

Baines cards. Ces cartes imprimées sur papier furent le résultat du premier projet commercial ingénieux né d´un sport populaire et tourné vers les masses. Sur le dos des cartes, vendues par paquets aux fans dans de petits magasins, était souvent imprimées des publicités.

Baines cards. Estas tarjetas imprimidas de papel fueron el primer proyecto brillante y comercial a nivel de masas surgido del deporte popular. El dorso de las tarjetas que se vendían en paquetes en tiendas pequeñas y se coleccionaban por los aficionados, se usaba con frequencia para la publicidad.

Baines cards. Diese gedruckten Karten waren das erste gelungene kommerzielle Projekt in Verbindung mit einem populären Massensport. Sie wurden als Serien paketweise verkauft und von den Fans gesammelt, die Rückseite enthielt oft Werbung.

WELL PLAYED

FOSSE

WELL SHOT

STOKE SWIFTS

ON THE BALL

BURTON SWIFTS

"Charge!" Chromolithograph from "Boys Own Paper", ca. 1900. This violent charge on the goalkeeper, to knock him and the ball into the net, has long been outlawed by rule changes.

«Charge!» Chromolitographie extraite de «Boys Own Paper» vers 1900. Les violentes charges contre le gardien de but pour forcer sa défense et mettre le ballon dans le filet sont depuis longtemps interdites dans les règlements.

"Charge!" Litografía de cromo de "Boys Own Paper" hacia 1900. Esta carga violenta contra el portero para empujarlo a él y también al balón en la red ha sido desterrada por cambios del reglamento.

„Attacke!" Chromolithographie aus „Boys Own Paper", ca. 1900. Der dargestellte gewaltsame Angriff auf den Torhüter, um ihn mit dem Ball ins Tor zu befördern, ist längst durch veränderte Regeln verboten.

PRESTON NORTH END.

WINNERS of the ENGLISH ASSOCIATION CHALLENGE CUP, and CHAMPIONS of the FOOTBALL LEAGUE, 1888-9.

"The Invincibles". Preston North End were the unbeaten champions of the Football League in its first season, 1888/89, and also won the F. A. Cup.

«The Invincibles», Preston North End furent les champions invaincus de la Ligue durant sa première saison, 1888/89 et remportèrent également la Coupe de l'Association.

"Los invencibles". Preston North End fueron los invencidos campeones de la liga de fútbol en su primera temporada, 1888/89, y ganaron también la copa de la F. A.

„Die Unbesiegbaren". Preston North End war der ungeschlagene Champion der Football-Liga in ihrer ersten Saison 1888/89, das Team gewann auch den FA Cup.

London vs. Sussex, 1891. Woodcut from "Illustrated Sporting & Dramatic News".

Londres contre Sussex, 1891. Gravure extraite de l' «Illustrated Sporting & Dramatic News».

London contra Sussex, 1891. Grabado en madera de "Illustrated Sporting & Dramatic News".

London – Sussex, 1891. Holzschnitt aus „Illustrated Sporting & Dramatic News".

Eton Field Game. Print from a painting
by Henry G. Brooks, 1890.

Eton Field Game. Reproduction d'une
peinture d'Henry G. Brooks, 1890.

Eton Field Game. Estampa según una
pintura de Henry G. Brooks, 1890.

Eton Field Game. Druck nach einem
Gemälde von Henry G. Brooks, 1890.

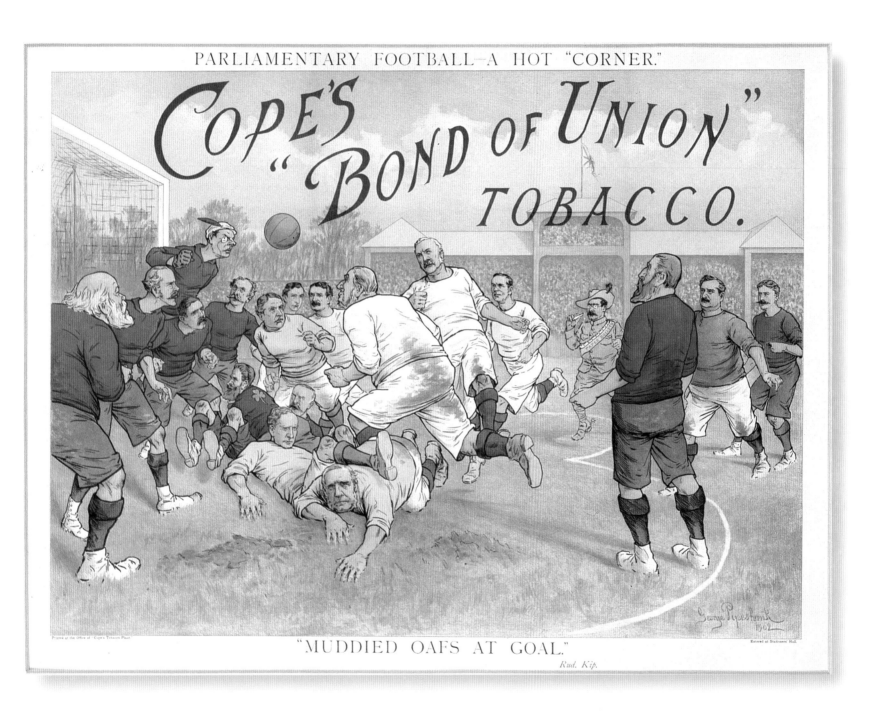

"Muddied Oafs". 1902 gravure print from a watercolor by "George Pipeshank" (John Wallace) illustrating a trade barriers argument with a soccer match metaphor.

«Muddied Oafs». 1902, gravure d´après une aquarelle de «George Pipeshank» (John Wallace), illustrant une polémique sur les tarifs douaniers à travers une métaphore tirée du football.

"Muddied Oafs". Grabado según una acuarela de "George Pipeshank" (John Wallace) de 1902 ilustrando el debate sobre barreras comerciales mediante una metáfora de un partido de fútbol.

„Schmutzige Lümmel". Diese Gravüre nach einem Aquarell von „George Pipeshank" (John Wallace), 1902, benutzt in der Debatte um Handelsschranken eine Fußballszene.

THE FOOTBALL ASSOCIATION PICTURE, (Key).

BY CHARLES H. PARKER. 17, NEW OXFORD STREET, W.C.

FINAL TIE.   **CRYSTAL PALACE PAVILION.**

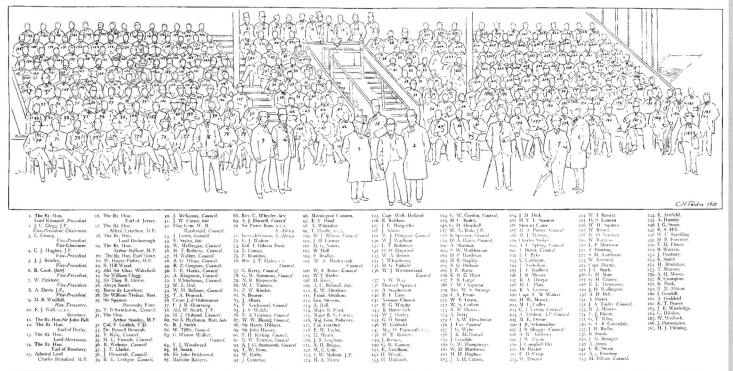

The Football Association Final, Crystal Palace Pavilion, 1910. Handcoloured engraving by Charles Barker with a key in separate frame.

Finale de L'association de football, Crystal Palace Pavilion, 1910. Gravure colorée à la main de Charles Barker avec une clé.

La final de la Asociación de Fútbol en Crystal Palace Pavilion, 1910. Grabado coloreado a mano de Charles Barker con los nombres correspondientes en un marco separado.

Endspiel um den FA Cup 1910, Crystal Palace Pavilion. Alle Honoratioren der Association sind abgebildet, mit einem entsprechenden Namensschlüssel. Handkolorierte Radierung von Charles Barker.

This book was published in 1905, cover by John Hassall, an early poster genius.

Ce livre fut publié en 1905, couverture par John Hassall, un des premiers maîtres affichistes.

Este libro fue publicado en 1905, cubierta de John Hassall, un antiguo maestro cartelista.

Dieses Buch erschien 1905, den Umschlag gestaltete John Hassall, ein früher Meister der Plakatkunst.

Football enters the song scene. Sheet music, early 20th century.

Le football fait son apparition dans le monde de la chanson . Partition du début du 20ème siècle.

El fútbol entra en la escena de las canciones. Partitura de principios del siglo XX.

Der Fußball betritt die Song-Szene. Schlager-Notenausgabe, Anfang 20. Jahrhundert.

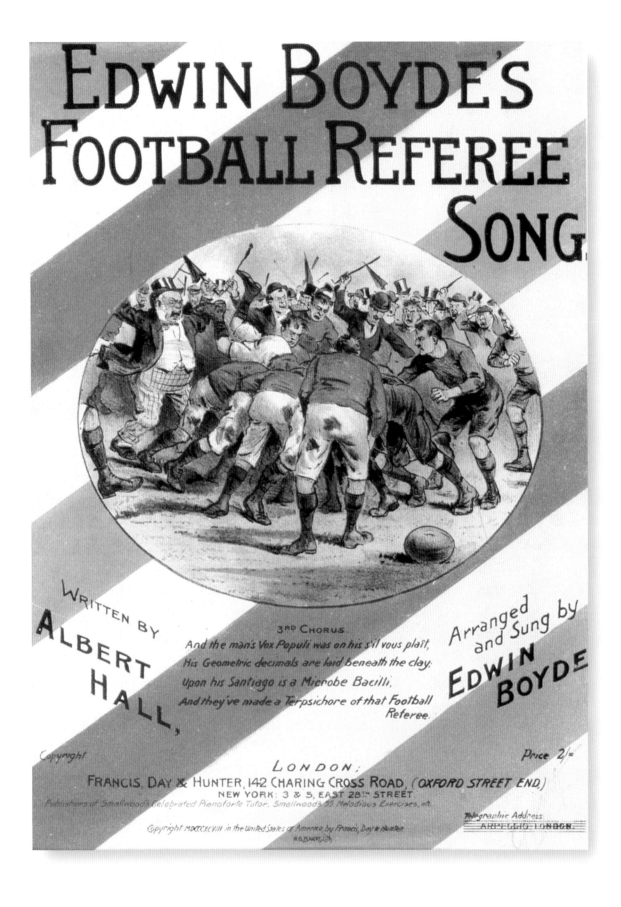

The Referee in song. Two early 20th century pieces of sheet music.

L´ arbitre en chanson. Deux morceaux du début du 20ème siècle sur partition.

El árbitro en las canciones. Dos ejemplares antiguos de partituras de principios del siglo XX.

Der Schiedsrichter als Schlager-Gegenstand. Zwei Notenausgaben, Anfang 20. Jahrhundert.

Chelsea F. C., 1905. A hand-coloured print of a team which included one of the biggest, fattest goalkeepers to play in the first-class game, "Fatty Foulkes".

Chelsea F. C., 1905. Illustration peinte à l a main d´une équipe qui comprenait l´une des plus grands et gras gardien de but à jouer en première division, «Fatty Foulkes».

Chelsea F. C., 1905. Estampa coloreada a mano de un equipo que incluía uno de los porteros más altos y más gordos que jamás jugó en un partido de primera clase, "Fatty Foulkes".

Chelsea F. C., 1905. Handkolorierter Druck, zum Team gehörte einer der längsten und dicksten Torhüter, der je in der 1. Liga spielte, „Fatty Foulkes".

Amateur tradition. This watercolour by Ernest Prater in 1913 shows the heyday of the amateur game when it lived sturdily alongside the professionals.

Tradition d´amateur. Cette aquarelle d´Ernest Prater de 1913 illustre la grande époque de l´amateurisme, lorsqu´il se maintenait parallèlement au jeu professionnel.

Tradición de los aficionados. Esta acuarela de Ernest Prater de 1913 muestra la cima del juego de aficionados cuando esta tradición coexistía con los profesionales.

Amateur-Tradition. Dieses Aquarell von Ernest Prater, 1913, stammt aus der Blütezeit des Amateurfußballs, als dieser noch völlig gleichrangig mit dem Profisport war.

Invicta Challenge Shield. London
elementary school trophy, 1890s.

Invicta Challenge Shield. Trophée de
l'école élémentaire de Londres vers
1895.

Invicta Challenge Shield. Trofeo
de una escuela primaria
de Londres, hacia 1895.

Invicta Challenge Shield, eine
Londoner Schultrophäe um 1895.

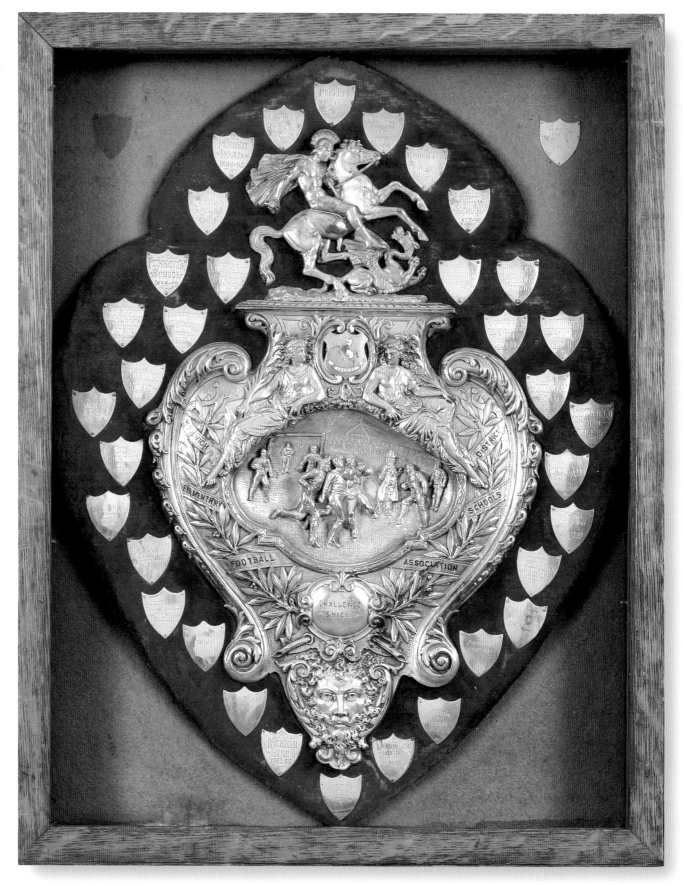

Early 20th century poster advertising "Boys Realm Paper".

Poster du début du 20ème siècle faisant de la publicité pour le «Boys Realm Paper».

Cartel de principios del siglo XX haciendo publicidad de "Boys Realm Paper".

Werbeplakat für „Boys Realm Paper", Anfang 20. Jahrhundert.

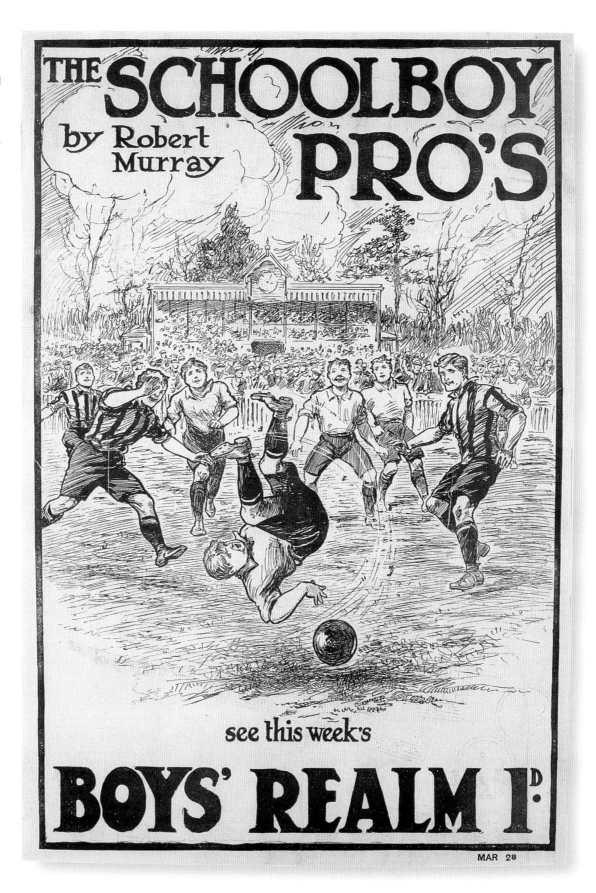

6 The World Joins in
Le phénomène s'étend au monde entier
Difusión mundial del fútbol
Die Welt schließt sich an

Britain likes to think that it gave Soccer to the world, and to a considerable extent this is true. First British teams toured as „ambassadors" of the new game in European countries. Football players were exported round the British Empire as sailors, soldiers, priests, administrators and traders. The Football they played was a rough mixture of old traditional games and the evolving new rules. In some countries it left an indelible sporting foundation. However, many nations were unimpressed by the restricting ideals of amateurism and the deeply-ingrained British love of rugged combat. In the long run, the Football that evolved in Europe and South America was more stylish and less physical than the original. Furthermore, the more ludicrous elements of high-amateurism were ignored.

Les Anglais aiment à penser qu'ils ont apporté au monde le «Soccer», ce qui est vrai en grande partie. Les premières équipes britanniques entreprirent des tournées en Europe comme ambassadrices de ce nouveau sport. Des joueurs furent dispersés à travers tout l'empire colonial britannique comme marins, soldats, prêtres, fonctionnaires ou négociants. Ils pratiquaient un football résultant d'un mélange indéfini entre le jeu traditionnel et les nouvelles règles. Dans certains pays ce style laissa des traces indélébiles. Cependant, certaines nations ne se montrèrent pas réceptives à l'idéal d'amateurisme ainsi qu'à l'amour des rudes combats profondément ancré dans le cœur britannique. A long terme, le style de football qui évolua en Europe et en Amérique du Sud, fut plus subtile et moins physique que l'original. On ignora par ailleurs les éléments les plus ridicules de cet amateurisme poussé à l'extrême.

A los britanos les gusta pensar que han regalado el fútbol al mundo, y hasta cierto punto tienen razón. Fueron equipos británicos, los que viajaron como „embajadores" del nuevo juego por Europa. Jugadores de fútbol fueron enviados a todo lo largo del Imperio Británico como marineros, soldados, sacerdotes, administradores, y comerciantes. El fútbol que jugaban era una mezcla ruda entre antiguo fútbol tradicional y las nuevas reglas. En algunos países dejaron una huella deportiva indeleble. Sin embargo, muchas naciones no se dejaron impresionar por los ideales restrictivos del fútbol aficionado británico y tampoco por aquel profundo y enraizado amor al combate duro. Con el tiempo, el fútbol que se desarrolló en Europa y en Sudamérica tuvo más estilo y menos fuerza física que el original. Además, los elementos más ridículos del fútbol aficionado fueron ignorados.

Großbritannien geht gern davon aus, daß es der Welt den Fußball gebracht hat, und zu einem erheblichen Teil stimmt das auch. Es waren erste britische Teams, die als „Botschafter" des neuen Spiels in europäischen Ländern auftraten. Es waren britische Seeleute, Soldaten, Geistliche, Beamte und Händler, die das Fußballspiel in das gesamte damalige Weltreich mitbrachten. Was sie spielten, war eine grobe Mischung aus alten traditionellen Formen und den eben entstandenen neuen Regeln. In einigen Ländern wurde damit der sportliche Grundstein gelegt. Viele Nationen blieben jedoch unbeeindruckt von den einengenden Idealen des Amateursports wie von der tiefverwurzelten britischen Vorliebe für den rauhen Kampf. Der Fußball, der sich schließlich in Europa und Südamerika entwickelte, wurde mit mehr Stil und weniger Kraft betrieben als das ursprüngliche britische Original. Und: Man ignorierte das extreme, eher komische Festhalten am strikten Amateurstandpunkt.

British teams as "ambassadors" in Europe. Tunbridge Wells on a Belgian tour vs. United Brussels, 1896.

Equipe britanniques comme «ambassadrice» en Europe. Tunbridge Wells lors d´une tournée en Belgique contre United Brussels, 1896.

Equipos británicos como "embajadores" en Europa. Tunbridge Wells contra United Bruselas durante un recorrido por Bélgica, 1896.

Britische Teams als „Botschafter" des neuen Spiels. Tunbridge Wells – United Brüssel, 1896.

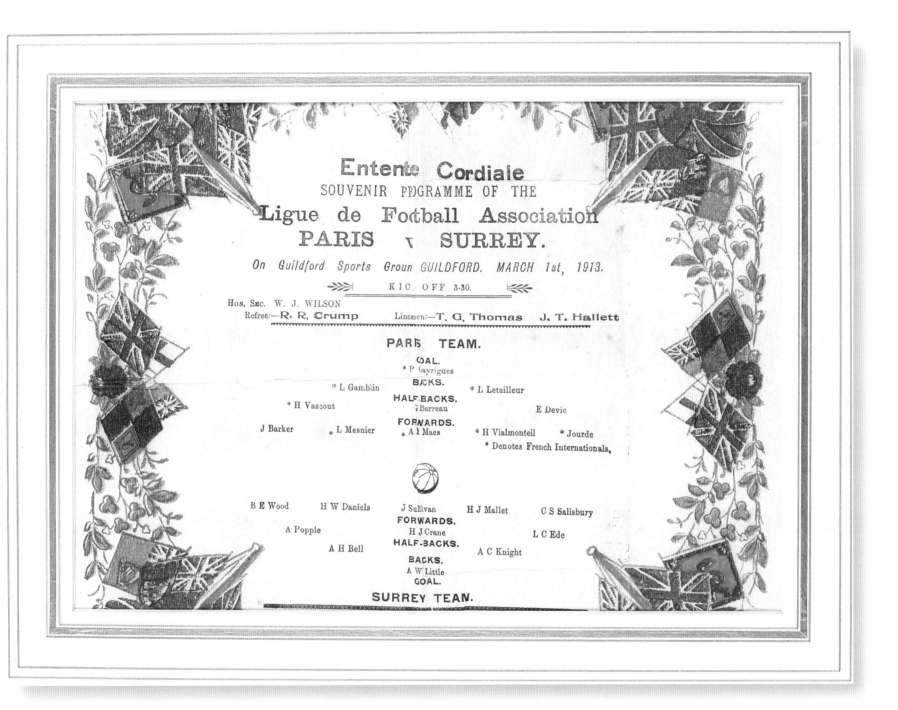

Paris vs. Surrey, 1913. Souvenir program.   Paris contre Surrey, 1913. Programme.   Paris contra Surrey, 1913. Programa.   Paris – Surrey, 1913. Programmzettel zum Spiel.

British players who influenced the early European Soccer.
James Richardson Spensley started Soccer in Italy in 1893 when he founded the Genoa Cricket and Football Club.

Joueurs anglais influencèrent le Soccer qui faisait son apparition en Europe. James Richardson Spensley introduisit le Soccer en Italie en 1893, lorsqu´il fonda le club cricket et de football de Gene.

Futbolistas británicos que influenciaron el fútbol europeo.
James Richardson Spensley empezó el fútbol en Italia en 1893 fundando el Club de Cricket y Fútbol de Génova.

Britische Spieler, die den frühen europäischen Fußball beeinflußten. James Richardson Spensley begründete das Spiel 1893 in Italien, als er den Cricket- und Fußballklub Genua ins Leben rief.

Jim Hogan embarked a lifetime career as a coach in Hungary, Germany and Austria.

Jim Hogan débuta une longue carrière comme entraîneur en Hongrie, Allemagne et Autriche.

Jim Hogan hizo toda su vida una carrera como entrenador en Hungria, Alemania y Austria.

Jim Hogan war jahrzehntelang als Trainer in Ungarn, Deutschland und Italien tätig.

Italy plunged wholeheartedly into the idea of organized Soccer, leagues and cups, from the last years of the 19th century. Milan and Turin were early rivals, as captured in this painting by Chris Jennings of a match in the Milan ground ninety years ago.

L'Italie s'engagea passionnément dans l'organisation de ligues et de coupes de Soccer dès la fin du 19ème siècle. Milan et Turin furent les premiers rivaux tel que le représente cette peinture de Chris Jennings lors d'un match à Milan il y a 90 ans.

Italia, ya desde los últimos años del siglo XIX, se entusiasmó con la idea del fútbol organizado, las ligas y copas. Milán y Turín fueron los primeros rivales como se ve en esta pintura de Chris Jennings de un partido en el campo de Milán hace 90 años.

Italien reagierte bereits gegen Ende des 19. Jahrhunderts begeistert auf die Idee des organisierten Fußballs mit Ligen und Cup-Wettbewerben. Mailand und Turin hießen die frühen Rivalen, wie auch auf diesem Gemälde von Chris Jennings, darstellend ein Match in Mailand vor neunzig Jahren.

Early Foot-Ball in France. Lithograph for the Paris satyrical magazine "L'Assiette au Beurre", 1902. One player says to another: "Brutish imbecile, idiot covered in mud. These are the terms given by the poet Kipling to he who plays at the savage Football. He will never be president of Racing!"

Début du Foot-Ball en France. Lithographie du magazine parisien satirique «L'Assiette au Beurre», 1902. Un joueur dit à un autre joueur: «Imbécile brutal, idiot couvert de boue. Ce sont les termes du poête Kipling décrivant les sauvages qui jouent au football. Il ne sera jamais président du Racing!»

Antiguo fútbol en Francia. Litografía para la revista satírica "L'Assiette au Beurre", 1902. Un futbolista dice al otro: "Bruto imbécil, idiota cubierto de mugre. Estas son las expresiones dadas por el poeta Kipling al que juega al fútbol bárbaro. El nunca será presidente del Racing!"

Früher Fußball in Frankreich. Lithographie für das satirische Pariser Magazin „L'Assiette au Beurre", 1902. Ein Spieler zum anderen: „Blöder Narr, schmutziger Lümmel – so bezeichnet der Dichter Kipling all jene, die das rohe Fußballspiel betreiben. Nun, der wird niemals Präsident von Racing Paris werden."

The celebrated Zeppelin over the cele-brated stadium . . . Wembley 1927.

Le fameux dirigable zeppelin au-dessus du fameux stade . . . Wembley 1927.

El celebrado cepelín encima del celebra-do estadio . . . Wembley 1927.

Der gefeierte Zeppelin über dem ge-feierten Stadion . . . Wembley 1927.

Two fine magazine covers for the Spanish language "Aire Libre", 1920s.

Deux jolies couvertures de magazine pour le journal hispanique «Aire Libre», 1920.

Dos cubiertas bonitas de la revista española "Aire Libre", de los años 1920.

Zwei schöne Umschlagzeichnungen aus den zwanziger Jahren, für das spanische Magazin „Aire Libre".

A ball at the battlefield. Calen Wood-ville print of World War I action – an actual bayonet charge where the British infantry kicked footballs ahead of them.

Une balle sur le champ de bataille. Représentation de Calen Woodville illustrant la première guerre mondiale.

Un balón en el campo de batalla. Estampa de Calen Woodville de un ataque de la infantería británica en la primera guerra mundial.

Ein Ball auf dem Schlachtfeld des Ersten Weltkriegs. Der Druck von Calen Woodville zeigt einen tatsächlichen Bajonettangriff der britischen Infanterie. Dabei trieb man Bälle vor sich her.

7 The Modern Era
L'ère contemporaine
La época moderna
Die moderne Ära

Round the world from the 1900s, new leagues and cup competitions were inaugurated with matching stadiums to house the growing millions of spectators. It was an unmatched phenomenon. British officials choked with moral indignation over the victories of Uruguay in the 1924 and 1928 Olympics, were convinced the South Americans were not snowy-white amateurs. Consequently, when the World Cup was inaugurated by the new "Federation Internationale de Football Association" (FIFA), and the first tournament awarded to Uruguay in 1930, no British teams took part. The split lasted 20 years. Europe's great teams of the 20s and 30s were Austria, Czechoslovakia and Italy. England finally lost their premier position in 1953 to perhaps the supreme European side, Hungary. And the flow of fine souvenirs embellishing the game now blossomed elsewhere.

Dès le début des années 1900, de nouvelles ligues et compétitions apparurent à travers le monde dans des stades de plus en plus impressionnants afin d'accueillir la foule grandissante des millions de spectateurs. Il s'agit d'un phénomène sans doute inégalé. Les officiels britanniques choqués et indignés moralement par les victoires successives de l'Uruguay aux jeux Olympiques de 1924 et 1928, étaient convaincus que les Sud Américains n'étaient pas des amateurs blancs comme neige. En conséquence, aucune équipe anglaise ne participa au premier tournoi qui eut lieu en Uruguay en 1930 lors de la coupe du monde inaugurée par la toute jeune «Federation Internationale de Football Association», la FIFA. La fracture dura vingt ans. Les grandes équipes européennes des années vingt et trente étaient autrichienne, tchécoslovaque et italienne. L'Angleterre céda finalement son titre de champion en 1953 à la Hongrie. Ainsi le flot de souvenirs embellissant le jeu, alla s'enrichir ailleurs.

A partir de 1900, las nuevas ligas y los campeonatos dieron lugar en todo el mundo a la inauguración de nuevos estadios para dar cabida a la creciente cantidad de espectadores – un fenómeno hasta esta época desconocido. Representantes británicos se llenaron de indignación por las victorias de Uruguay en los Juegos Olímpicos de 1924 y 1928, pues estaban convencidos que los sudamericanos no eran simples aficionados. En consecuencia, los equipos británicos no tomaron parte cuando la nueva "Federation Internationale de Football Association" (FIFA) creó el Campeonato Mundial de Fútbol, cuyo primer torneo se hizo en 1930 en Uruguay. Esta ausencia duró 20 años. Los grandes equipos europeos de los años 20 y 30 fueron Austria, Checoslovaquia e Italia. Inglaterra perdió, finalmente, su supremacía en 1953, ante la quizás más poderosa Hungría. Por todas partes surgieron también una serie de hermosos objetos recordatorios embelleciendo los juegos.

Ab 1900 wurden in aller Welt neue Liga- und Cup-Wettbewerbe eingeführt, dazu entstanden beeindruckende Stadien, um die wachsende Millionenzahl der Zuschauer aufnehmen zu können – ein bis dahin unbekanntes Phänomen. Als Uruguay die olympischen Fußballturniere von 1924 und 1928 gewann, waren britische Offizielle davon überzeugt, daß es sich bei den Südamerikanern nicht um blütenreine Amateure handeln könne, und reagierten mit moralischer Entrüstung. Als dann der eben gegründete Weltverband „Federation Internationale de Football Association" (FIFA) die erste Weltmeisterschaft 1930 an Uruguay vergab, nahmen keine britischen Teams daran teil. Dieser Boykott sollte 20 Jahre anhalten. Die großen europäischen Mannschaften der zwanziger und dreißiger Jahre waren Österreich, die Tschechoslowakei und Italien. Danach nahm England die führende Position ein, bis zur Niederlage 1953 im legendären Spiel gegen Ungarn. Das Geschäft mit Souvenirs rund um den Fußball aber blühte in allen Ländern gleichermaßen.

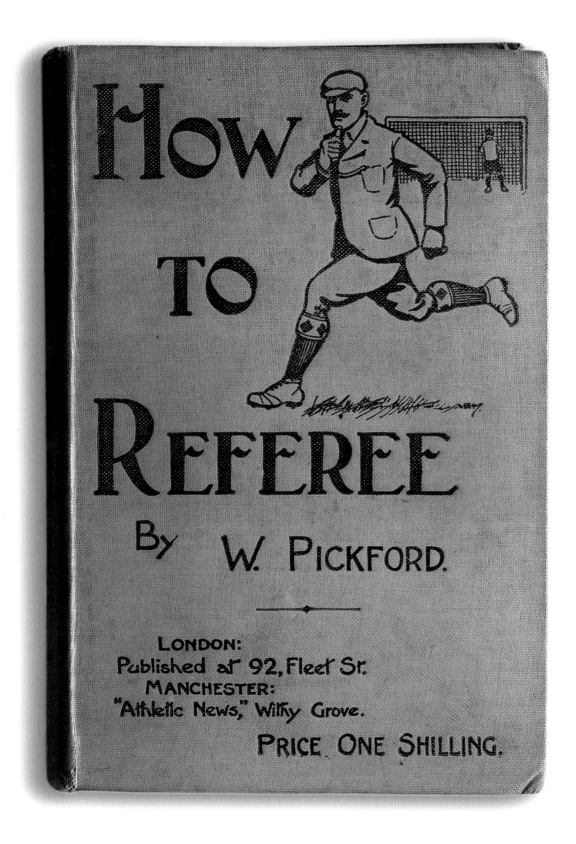

This book was published in 1906 and shows how distinctively referees dressed in early days. Not good for Aztec Stadium at high noon!

Ce livre fut publié en 1906 et nous montre la forme d'habillement des arbitres aux vieux temps du jeu.

Este libro fue publicado en 1906 y muestra la manera de vestir de los árbitros en los tiempos antiguos del juego.

Dieses Buch erschien 1906 und zeigt, wie die Schiedsrichter in den frühen Tagen des Spiels gekleidet waren.

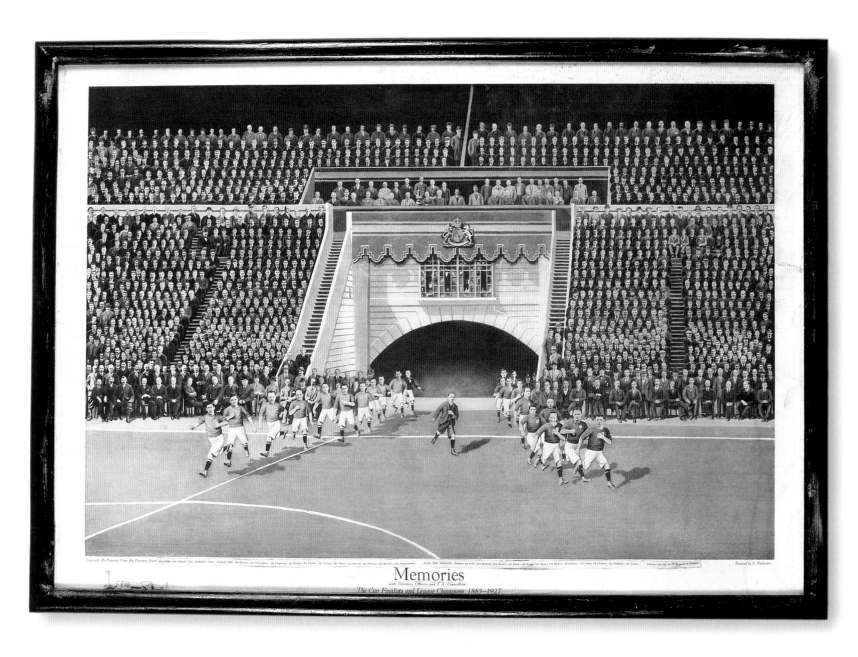

Memories
with Directors, Officers and F.A. Councillors
The Cup Finalists and League Champions 1883–1927

1927 collage of FA Cup Final teams Arsenal and Cardiff City running out at Wembley with the stand behind them full of all the players in all the teams to have won the Cup or League since 1893.

1927, montage représentant les équipes de l'Arsenal et de Cardiff City finalistes de la Coupe d l'Association. Sur ce montage les deux équipes se rencontrent au stade de Wembley, dont les tribunes sont remplies de joueurs de toutes origines ayant déjà remporté la Coupe ou la Ligue depuis 1893.

Montaje de los equipos finalistas Arsenal y Cardiff City 1927 entrando en el campo de Wembley detrás la tribuna llena de futbolistas de todos los equipos que habían ganado la copa o la liga desde 1893.

Endspiel um den FA Cup 1927, Collage. Die Teams von Arsenal London und Cardiff City beim Einlaufen in das Wembley-Stadion. Auf den Tribünen dahinter die Spieler sämtlicher Mannschaften, die den Cup seit 1893 gewonnen hatten.

Once again Aston Villa, now in the season 1937/38.

Une fois encor Aston Villa, cette fois-çi durant la saison 1937/38.

Otra vez Aston Villa, ahora en la temporada de 1937/38.

Noch einmal Aston Villa, hier in der Saison 1937/38.

West Bromwich skipper meets King George V. Oils on board by J. Higgs, 1932.

Le capitaine West Bromwich rencontre le roi George V d'après J. Higgs, huile de 1932.

El jefe del equipo West Bromwich se encuentra con el rey George V. Oleo sobre tabla de J. Higgs, 1932.

König George V. begrüßt den Kapitän von West Bromwich. Ölgemälde von J. Higgs, 1932.

"The Tackle". Czechoslovakian, early 20th century, electro-plated bronze group of two players challenging for a gigantic many-panelled ball.

«La prise du ballon». Tchécoslovaquie, début du 20ème siècle, bronze représentant deux joueurs se disputant un ballon énorme à plusieurs facettes.

"The Tackle". Checoslovaco, principios del siglo XX, grupo cubierto de bronce electricamente de dos futbolistas luchando por un balón gigante compuesto de muchas piezas.

„Tackling". Bronzegruppe zweier Spieler im Kampf um einen gigantischen Ball, Tschechoslowakei, Anfang 20. Jahrhundert.

Two polished Austrian bronzes of distinctive style by the Austrian sculptor and medallist, Adolph Wagner von der Muhl, early 1920s.

Deux bronzes polis australiens de style distinct du sculpteur et médailliste austrien Adolph Wagner von der Muhl, au début des années 1920.

Dos bronces austríacos pulimentados de estilo pronunciado del escultor y medallista austríaco Adolph Wagner von der Muhl, principios de los años XX.

Zwei polierte Bronzestatuetten des österreichischen Bildhauers Adolph Wagner von der Muhl, Anfang 20. Jahrhundert.

OLYMPIA - HOLLANDIAAN 5 - 2
GOUDA, 17 SEPTEMBER 1933.

OLYMPIA	DE HOLLANDIAAN
V. HENRIQUER	P. H. ODIJK
G. DE JONG	F. BEEKHUYZEN
W. v. TILBURG	D. v. d. KNAAP
B. HAGENDIJK	A. v. d. ROEST
G. VLOT	G. PRINS
H. v. ZUTPHEN	P. A. BAKKER
R. v. d. HENDE	M. TERMYN
W. MALLON	C. DE ROND
E. KROM	P. v. d. ROEST
M. BIK	C. HOFMAN
L. HORNEMAN	L. v. WOERKOM

N.O.A.D. - WILLEM II 0 - 1
TILBURG, 24 SEPTEMBER 1933.

N.O.A.D.	WILLEM II
H. v. TILBURG	L. v. d. AA
J. v. PELT	A. v. IERLAND
J. JANSEN	N. v. HAM
M. DE KOK	H. DE LEEUW
A. OPRINSEN	F. v. d. POEL
C. BERTENS	G. MOLLER
P. BOLSIUS	PH. TAMINIAU
A. WITTERS	G. HERMANS
C. REMMERS	J. v. d. WOUW
W. FRANKEN	M. MAAS
H. v. HAZENDONK	AUG. SMULDERS

Two pages from a large Dutch album issued by "Miss Blanche cigarettes" with glossy action photographs from the seasons 1933/34 in enhanced colour.

Deux pages extraites d'un album hollandais publié dans «Miss Blanche cigarette» avec les photographies en couleur des meilleures actions de la saison 1933/34.

Dos páginas de un álbum voluminoso editado por "Miss Blanche cigarettes" con brillantes fotos de acción de las temporadas de 1933/34.

Zwei Seiten aus einem holländischen Zigarettenbilder-Album der Firma „Miss Blanche", mit schönen kolorierten Fotos von Spielen der Saison 1933/34.

"The Goalkeeper". Powerful British 1930s image of a professional goalkeeper in front of a massive crowd, signed J. Petts.

«Le gardien de but». Image anglaise des années 1930 peine de force représentant un gardien de but professionnel face à une troupe massive signée J. Petts.

"El guardameta". Imagen británica expresiva de los años 1930 de un guardameta profesional delante de una muchedumbre densa, firmado por J. Petts.

„Der Torhüter". Eindrucksvolle britische Darstellung aus den dreißiger Jahren, von J. Petts.

"Big Match". A large British commercial painting, water colour and poster paint by the English poster artist Septimus Edwin Scott, early 1950s.

«Le grand match». Grande peinture commerciale anglaise en aquarelle, et poster réalisé par l'artiste anglais Septimus Edwin Scott au début des années 1950.

"Gran partido". Una pintura comercial grande de Gran Bretaña, acuarela y colores de carteles del artista británico de carteles Septimus Edwin Scott, principios de los años 50.

„Ein großes Spiel". Britisches Werbebild in Aquarell- und Plakatfarbe von Septimus Edwin Scott, Anfang der fünfziger Jahre.

"Penalty". A French watercolour by Paul Onduer used as front cover for the France Football magazine 1955.

«Penalty». Aquarelle française de Paul Onduer utilisée comme couverture pour le magazine de football français de 1955.

"Penalty". Una acuarela francesa de Paul Onduer usada como cubierta para la revista francesa de fútbol 1955.

„Elfmeter". Aquarell von Paul Onduer, Umschlagbild für das französische Fußballmagazin, 1955.

British Sheet music from the beginning of the "roaring twenties".

Une partition anglaise du début des années vingt enflammées.

Partitura británica, del principio de los años 20 "de oro".

Britische Schlager-Ausgabe vom Beginn der „Goldenen zwanziger Jahre".

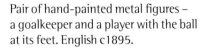

Pair of hand-painted metal figures – a goalkeeper and a player with the ball at its feet. English c1895.

Paire de figurines de métal peintes à la main – un gardien de but et un joueur avec le ballon au pied. Angleterre, années 1930.

Dos figuras de metal coloreadas a mano – un guardameta y un jugador con el balón en el pie. Inglaterra, años 1930.

Ein Paar handbemalter Metallfiguren – ein Torhüter und ein Spieler mit Ball am Fuß. England, um 1895.

"ROWLEY."

Framed Vanity Fair type portrait prints of Cambridge University soccer players, circa 1900.

Portraits de footballeurs populaires du Cambridge University, vers 1900.

Estampas de retratos de futbolistas conocidos de la universidad de Cambridge, alrededor de 1900.

Porträtdrucke bekannter Fußballspieler der Cambridge University, ca. 1900.

J. E. Doig (Sunderland)
"Saving a goal".

J. Goodall (Derby county)
"Breasting the ball."

Stanley Briggs (Clapton).

W. C. Athersmith (Aston Villa)
"Heading the ball".

G. O. Smith (Corinthians).

W. Bassett (West Bromwich Albion).

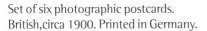

Set of six photographic postcards.
British,circa 1900. Printed in Germany.

Série de cartes postales photographiques
dans les années 1900. Britannique,
imprimé en Allemagne.

Serie de postales fotográficas. Inglaterra,
alrededor de 1900, impresas en Alemania.

Serie von photographischen Postkarten.
England ca. 1900, gedruckt in Deutschland.

Wembley Stadium on big match day.

Stade de Wembley par une journée de
match important.

El estadio Wembley en el día de un
juego importante.

Das Wembley-Stadion am Tag eines
großen Spiels.

Men of Mettle

JOHN F. SHAW & C° LONDON.

"Men of Mettle". Book title based on Shakespeare line "A Corinthian, a lad of mettle, a good boy". British, circa 1900.

«Hommes avec ferveur». Le titre de ce livre britannique vers 1900 fait référence au vers de Shakespeare «Un Corinthien, un gaillard avec ferveuer, un bon garçon.»

"Hombres con fervor". Título de un libro británico, hacia 1900, que se refiere al verso de Shakespeare "Un corintio, un joven con fervor, un buen muchacho."

„Männer mit Feuereifer". Der Titel dieses britischen Buches um 1900 nimmt Bezug auf Shakespeares Verszeile „Ein Korinther, ein Bursche mit Feuereifer, ein guter Junge."

Set of six football action postcards. English, 1905.

Série de cartes postales. Britannique, 1905.

Serie de postales inglesas, 1905.

Britische Postkartenserie, 1905.

A THROW IN.

A SPILL.

A SOUND DEFENCE.

WELL CLEARED.

A NEAT PASS.

GOAL.

8 Women and Football
Les femmes et le football
Las mujeres y el fútbol
Frauen und Fußball

The role of women in Football and the illustration of that role says more about men than their opposite numbers.

The first women teams were formed in 1880s in England, with Nettie Honeyball as a driving force.

But, for its first seventy or eighty years of the organized sport, women's matches were too often restricted to rare "charitable" events where men could gawp and giggle. Those days have gone. The days of crowds containing 40.000 flat caps and perhaps two brave bonnets have also gone ... almost.

Today modern soccer for women is serious and athletic and well worth watching with strong leagues round the world, and a successful World Cup.

Le rôle de la femme dans le football ainsi que son illustration, en dit plus long sur les hommes que sur les femmes elles-mêmes. Les premières équipes féminines furent formées en Angleterre dans les années 1880 sous l'impulsion de Nettie Honeyball.

Pourtant, les matchs d'équipes féminines furent relégués au rang d'évènements charitables où les hommes s'exclamaient et ricanaient durant les 70 à 80 premières années d'éxistence du football féminin comme discipline reconnue. Cette époque est désormais révolue, ainsi que celle où l'on comptait 40.000 hommes pour peut être deux courageuses femmes dans la foule des supporters ... ou presque.

De nos jours, le football féminin moderne est sérieux, athlétique, et bien encadré de par le monde par des ligues puissantes, et possède une brillante coupe du monde.

El papel de las mujeres en el fútbol y el análisis de este papel nos revela más acerca de los hombres que del sexo contrario. El primer equipo de mujeres fue formado en 1880 en Inglaterra, y su propulsora fue Nettie Honeyball.

Pero en los primeros 70 u 80 años de su organización, los partidos de mujeres fueron muy a menudo restringidos a eventos estrictamente "caritativos", donde los hombres podían mirar con la boca abierta y reírse. Esos son tiempos pasados. Aquellos días, en los que entre 40.000 espectadores solo había un par de mujeres, son cosas del pasado ... casi. Hoy en día, el fútbol femenino es algo serio y atlético, con bien organizadas ligas a lo largo de todo el mundo, y con un exitoso campeonato mundial.

Die Rolle der Frau im Fußball und die Belege für diese Rolle sagen mehr über die Männer aus als die tatsächlichen Spielerzahlen pro Geschlecht.

Erste Frauenmannschaften entstanden nach 1880 in England, mit Nettie Honeyball als treibender Kraft. Doch in den ersten siebzig bis achtzig Jahren des organisierten Fußballsports blieben Frauenspiele allzuoft seltene Ereignisse der „Nächstenliebe", bei denen die zuschauenden Männer kichern und lästern konnten. Diese Tage sind nun glücklicherweise vorbei. Vorbei – fast – sind auch die Tage, da sich unter 40.000 Zuschauern vielleicht zwei mutige Frauen befanden.

Frauenfußball wird heute ernsthaft, athletisch und anerkannt betrieben, mit eigenen Ligen in aller Welt und mit einer erfolgreichen eigenen Weltmeisterschaft.

Set of womens football kit , 1895,
and a painted plaster figure from 1900.

Equipements de football pour femmes,
1895 et visage en platre peint de 1900.

Equipo futbolístico para mujeres, 1895,
y una figura de yeso pintada de 1900.

Ein Satz Frauen-Spielkleidung von
1895 und eine bemalte Gipsfigur
von 1900.

Nettie Honeyball was the driving force
for women's football in the mid 1880s.

Nettie Honeyball était la «force vive»
du football féminin vers le milieu des
années 1880.

Nettie Honeyball era la fuerza motriz
del fútbol de mujeres en los años 80 del
siglo XIX.

Nettie Honeyball, die treibende Kraft
bei der Entstehung des Frauen-Fußballs
um 1885.

Pair of black Victorian girl's boots,
used with women's football, 1890.

Paire de bottines noires pour femmes
de l'époque Victorienne utilisée dans
le football féminin, 1890.

Un par de botas negras de la época
Victoriana usadas en el fútbol
femenino, 1890.

Ein Paar schwarze victorianische
Schuhe, wie sie um 1890 beim
Frauen-Fußball benutzt wurden.

THE
British Ladies' Football Club.

President—LADY FLORENCE DIXIE.

THE FIRST LADIES'
FOOTBALL MATCH
(NORTH v. SOUTH)

WILL BE PLAYED ON

Saturday, 23rd March, 1895,

UPON THE

CROUCH END ATHLETIC GROUND,

NIGHTINGALE LANE, HORNSEY.

KICK OFF 4.30.

The Ladies' Match will be preceded by

CROUCH END v. 3rd GRENADIER GUARDS,

KICK OFF 3 O'CLOCK.

Admission (including both Matches) 1s.

Covered Stand, 1s. extra.

Frequent Trains from Moorgate Street, Broad Street, King's Cross, and intermediate stations to Hornsey.

Ladies desirous of joining the above Club should apply to Miss NETTIE J. HONEYBALL, "Ellesmere," 27, Weston Park, Crouch End, N.

Footballs by COOK.   Caps by A. E. RAISIN, of Stroud Green Road.

W. & W. J. Mizen, Printers, 13, Stroud Green Road, N.

Original pamphlet for a 1895 women's match.

Pamphlet à l'occasion d'un match féminin en 1895.

Folleto original para un partido femenino de 1895.

Ankündigung eines Frauen-Spiels, 1895.

Original drawing by A. S. Boyd, 1890s, designed to get a negative reaction from London magazine's society readers.

Déssin original de A. S. Boyd, années 1890, fait pour causer de réactions negatives concernant le football féminin entre les lecteurs de société du magazine londonien.

Dibujo original de A. S. Boyd, hacia 1890, hecho con la intención de causar reacciones negativas frente al fútbol femenino entre los lectores de la revista londinense provenientes de la alta sociedad.

Originalzeichnung von A. S. Boyd, um 1890, entstanden in der Absicht, bei den gehobenen Lesern des Londoner Magazins negative Reaktionen zum Frauenfußball zu erzeugen.

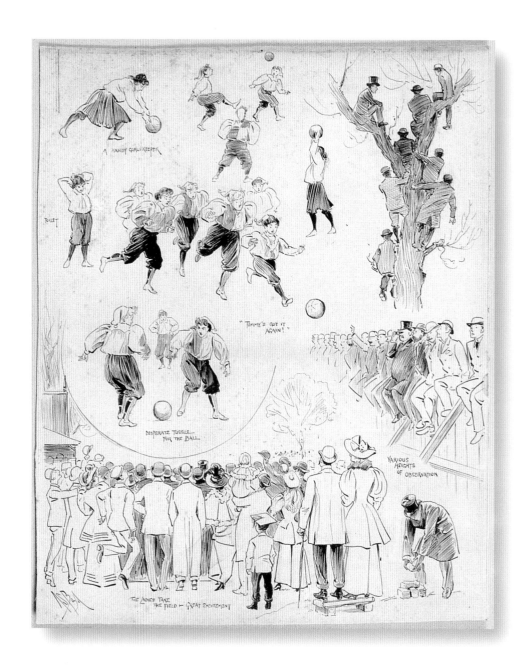

Montage from a soccer scrapbook, late 1890s.

Montage à partir d´un album de football, fin des années 1890.

Montaje de un álbum coleccionable, final de los años 90 del siglo XIX.

Montage aus einem Fußball-Erinnerungsbuch, ca. 1890.

The two teams and a newspaper report about a women's Football match in Edinburgh, 1881.

Les deux équipes d'un match fémimin disputé à Edinburgh et coupures de presse, 1881.

Los dos equipos y un reportaje de un periódico sobre un partido entre mujeres en Edinburgo 1881.

Frauen-Fußballmatch in Edinburgh, 1881. Die beiden Teams sowie ein Zeitungsbericht vom Spiel.

Miss Lynn.   Miss Honeyball.   Miss Williams.   Miss Edwards.   Miss Ide.
Miss Couyland.   Miss Fenn.   Miss Gilbert.   Miss Smith.   Miss Thiers.   Miss Biggs.
THE LADY FOOTBALLERS: NORTH TEAM.
FROM A PHOTOGRAPH BY SYMMONS AND THIELE, CHANCERY LANE, W.C.

Miss Hicks.   Miss Clarke.   Miss A. Hicks.   Miss Edwards.   Miss Clarence.
Miss Lewis.   Miss Roberts.   Miss Ellie.   Miss Lewis.   Miss Fenn.
THE LADY FOOTBALLERS: SOUTH TEAM.
FROM A PHOTOGRAPH BY SYMMONS AND THIELE, CHANCERY LANE, W.C.

FOOTBALL.

MATCH BY WOMEN IN EDINBURGH.

So it has come at last! What next? Two teams of young women have just played a game under Association Rules in Edinburgh. Several years ago there was a rage for silly displays of certain kinds of athletics by women, but we thought the time had passed for another outburst in the form of Association football. It had been whispered some weeks ago that twenty-two young women were practising the dribbling game in a hall in Glasgow for the purpose of "coming out," and that eventually they had applied to several of the Glasgow clubs for the use of their ground, but not one would grant it for such a purpose. Somehow or other, however, the Edinburgh Association players are not so particular about the arrangement of matches, if there is any chance of a gate, and the ground at Eastern Road belonging to the Hibernians was given without much ado. To give the arrangement the semblance of an international event the girls had the "cheek" to designate the farce, England v Scotland, and, as a matter of course, it suited them best to allow Scotland to win by three goals to none. The "Scotch Eleven" wore blue jerseys, with crimson sashes round the waist, knickerbockers, blue and white hose, and high laced boots, while the English team had on crimson jerseys, with blue sashes, white knickerbockers, and crimson and white hose, and badges with the English lion. The football shown was of the most primitive order, and reminded one of a couple of A B C classes of schoolboys engaged in a "big side." It is said that other matches are about to come off, one in Glasgow this afternoon. If it does come off in that city it will most probably be on some of the professional running grounds, for no football club with any regard for its good name would encourage such a humiliating spectacle made of the popular winter pastime. The names of the women who played in the game are as follows:—

SCOTLAND.—Miss Ethel Hay (goal), Bella Oswald and Georgina Wright (backs), Rose Rayman and Isa Stevenson (half backs), Emma Wright, Louise Cole, Lilly St Clair, Maud Riweford, Carrie Baliol, and Minnie Brymner (forwards).

ENGLAND.—Miss May Goodwin (goal), Mabel Bradbury and Maud Hopewell (backs), Maud Starling and Ada Everston (half backs), Geraldine Vintner, Mabel Vance, Eva Davenport, Minnie Hopewell, Kate Mellon, and Nelly Sherwood (forwards).

Early cards of girl footballers, 1906.

Premières cartes postales représentants des joueuses de football, 1906.

Tarjetas primitivas de muchachas jugando al fútbol, principios del siglo XX.

Frühe Postkarten fußballspielender Mädchen, 1906.

HALF-TIME

DICK, KERR'S LADIES' FOOTBALL TEAM.

The Wallsend women's team
with its male coach, 1917.

L'équipe féminine de Wallsend
avec son entraîneur masculin, 1917.

El equipo de mujeres de Wallsend
con su entrenador masculino, 1917.

Die Frauenmannschaft von Wallsend
mit ihrem Trainer, 1917.

Gouache of French showgirl high kicking a colourful football, early 1920s.

Gouache d´une artiste de cabaret française frappant de toutes ses forces dans un ballon de football de toutes les couleurs, début des années 1920.

Acuarela de una artista de revista que lanza un balón de muchos colores en el aire, principios de los años 20.

Ein Showgirl mit Fußball, französische Gouache vom Anfang der zwanziger Jahre.

Some more early cards of girl foot-ballers, 1906.

Premières cartes postales représentants des joueuses de football, 1906.

Más tarjetas de futbolistas femeninas del año 1906.

Noch einige frühe Postkarten, 1906.

A FOOTBALL MATCH!

OH! WHAT A GAME IT IS

A FINE ALL-ROUND PLAYER.

PLAYING THE GAME WITH THE BOYS.

MAKING UP FOR THE OTHER PLAYERS.

9 Playing equipment
L'équipement
Implementos del juego
Spielausrüstung

When Charles Goodyear, the American inventor, won a gold medal for his rubber Football at the international exhibition in Paris in 1854, he didn't know he was about to revolutionize sports and games. Rubber-cored playballs (plain rubber was too bouncy) would change the shape of Golf, Tennis and Football more than any other single factor. By the 1870s, factories had sprung up across Britain where not only balls were manufactured cheaply for mass sales, but also various other kinds of equipment for the new game – caps, playing strip (knitted jerseys and long baggy "shorts"), socks, boots and shinguards.

At the same time a large industry started for honours caps, Football colours, badges of honour and various kinds of national and club badges.

Lorsque l'inventeur américain, Charles Goodyear, remporta une médaille d'or pour son ballon de football en caoutchouc à l'Exposition Universelle de Paris en 1854, il ne se doutait pas qu'il était sur le point de révolutionner sports et jeux. Ces balles dont l'intérieur était en caoutchouc (des balles entièrement en caoutchouc rebondissaient trop), allaient modifier la physionomie du golf, du tennis et du football plus que toute autre invention. A partir des années 1870, des usines furent implantées en Grande Bretagne, où l'on y produisait non seulement des ballons bon marché pour les masses, mais aussi d'autres équipements variés pour le nouveau jeu: casquettes, tenues de jeu (maillots ajourés et larges shorts), chaussettes, chaussures et protège-tibias.

À la même période une industrie parallèle importante apparut, spécialisée dans les casquettes de prestige, les ballons de couleur, les badges honorifiques et diverses sortes de badges nationaux ou de clubs.

Cuando Charles Goodyear, el inventor norteamericano, ganó una medalla de oro por su pelota de goma en la Exposición Universal de París en 1854, no sabía que iniciaba una revolución en el deporte y en los juegos. Pelotas con un interior de goma (pues de pura goma rebotarían demasiado) cambiarían la forma del golf, del tenis y del fútbol más que cualquier otro factor. A partir de 1870, surgieron fábricas a todo lo largo de Gran Bretaña, donde no solamente se producían pelotas a bajo precio para un consumo masivo, sino también un sinúmero de otros implementos para el nuevo juego: gorras, ropa deportiva (camisetas de punto y anchos pantalones cortos), medias, botas de fútbol y espinilleras.

Al mismo tiempo surgió una gran industria de gorras y escudos distintivos tanto de los clubes como de los paises.

Als der amerikanische Erfinder Charles Goodyear 1854 auf der Weltausstellung in Paris für seinen Fußball aus Gummi eine Goldmedaille gewann, ahnte er nicht, daß er damit fast alle sportlichen Spiele revolutionieren würde. Bälle mit Gummikern (reiner Gummi war zu elastisch) sollten künftig Golf, Tennis und Fußball stärker verändern als jeder andere Faktor.

Ab 1870 schossen in ganz Großbritannien Fabriken aus dem Boden, die nicht nur preiswerte Bälle für den Massenbedarf produzierten, sondern auch verschiedenste andere Ausrüstungen für das neue Spiel – Mützen, Spielkleidung (Strickjerseys und lange bauschige „Shorts"), Strümpfe, Schuhe und Schienbeinschützer.

Gleichzeitig entstand eine bedeutende Industrie für Fankappen, Aufnäher, Abzeichen sowie die verschiedensten nationalen und klubeigenen Fußball-Insignien.

Decorative caps of the 19th and early 20th century, typical for the fine quality of these awards by British Clubs.

Couvre-chefs décoratifs du 19ème et du début du 20ème siècle dont le raffinement est caractéristique des récompenses données par les clubs britanniques.

Gorras decorativas del siglo XIX y de principios del siglo XX, típicos para la alta calidad de estos premios de clubs británicos.

Dekorative Kappen, Ende 19./ Anfang 20. Jahrhundert. Deutlich wird die hervorragende Qualität dieser britischen Klub-Insignien.

England v. Ireland 1911, all white official velvet cap with gold embroidered rose.

Angleterre contre Irlande 1911, couvre-chef de cérémonie en velour blanc avec une rose brodée à l'or fin.

Inglaterra contra Irlanda 1911, gorra oficial de terciopelo blanco con rosa bordada en oro.

England – Irland, 1911. Die offizielle weiße Samtmütze zu diesem Länderspiel, mit der goldgestickten Rose.

Irish cap, green velvet with gold braid and tassel, awarded to Manchester United star Johnny Carey.

Beret irelandais en velour vert avec fil d'or et pompon offert en récompense à la vedette du Manchester United, Johny Carey.

Gorra irlandesa de terciopelo verde con ribete de oro y borla, recompensa a la estrella de Manchester United, Johnny Carey.

Irische Kappe aus grünem Samt, mit Goldborte und Quaste, getragen von Manchester United-Star Johnny Carey.

FOOTBALL COLOURS OF SOME OF OUR PUBLIC SCHOOLS

AMPLEFORTH · BEDFORD · BRIGHTON · CANFORD · CHARTERHOUSE · CHELTENHAM · CHRIST'S HOSPITAL · CLIFTON · CRANLEIGH · DOVER · DOWNSIDE

DULWICH · EASTBOURNE · ETON (FIELD) · ETON (RUGBY) · FETTES · GLENALMOND · HAILEYBURY · HARROW · HIGHGATE · LANCING · LEYS

LLANDOVERY · LORETTO · MALVERN · MARLBOROUGH · MERCHANT TAYLORS' · MERCHISTON · MILL HILL · PORTORA · RADLEY · REPTON · ROSSALL

RUGBY · ST PAUL'S · SEDBERGH · SHERBORNE · SHREWSBURY · STOWE · TONBRIDGE · UPPINGHAM · WELLINGTON · WESTMINSTER · WINCHESTER

74 BOUVERIE STREET, LONDON E.C.

MORE FOOTBALL COLOURS OF OUR PUBLIC SCHOOLS

Football colours of some British Public Schools. From "Boys Own Paper", 1925.

Couleurs de l'équipe de football de certaines écoles britanniques. Extrait de "Boys Own Paper", 1925.

Colores de fútbol de unas escuelas privadas británicas. De "Boys Own Paper", 1925.

Mannschafts-Ausrüstung verschiedener britischer Public Schools. Aus „Boys Own Paper", 1925.

Various medal ribbons, silver medals and ornate badges, 19th and 20th century.

Divers rubans de médailles, médailles en argent et badges ornementaux du 19ème et 20ème siècle.

Varias cintas de medallas, medallas de plata e insignias decorativas siglos XIX y XX.

Auswahl von Medaillen, Aufnähern und Abzeichen, 19. und 20. Jahrhundert.

Four ornate gold wire and cloth Football Association badges, 1898-1905.

Quatre ficelles d´or ornementales et badges de l´Association de Football, 1898–1905.

Cuatro insignias decorativas de alambre de oro y tela de la Asociación de Fútbol, 1898-1905.

Vier goldbestickte und reich geschmückte Aufnäher der Football Association, 1898 –1905.

Set of women's football kit: socks, two hats and belt, 1906.

Equipement de football féminin: chaussettes, deux chapeaux et ceintures, 1906.

Equipo futbolístico para mujeres: calcetines, dos sombreros y un cinturón 1906.

Frauen-Spielkleidung von 1906: Strümpfe, zwei Mützen und Gürtel.

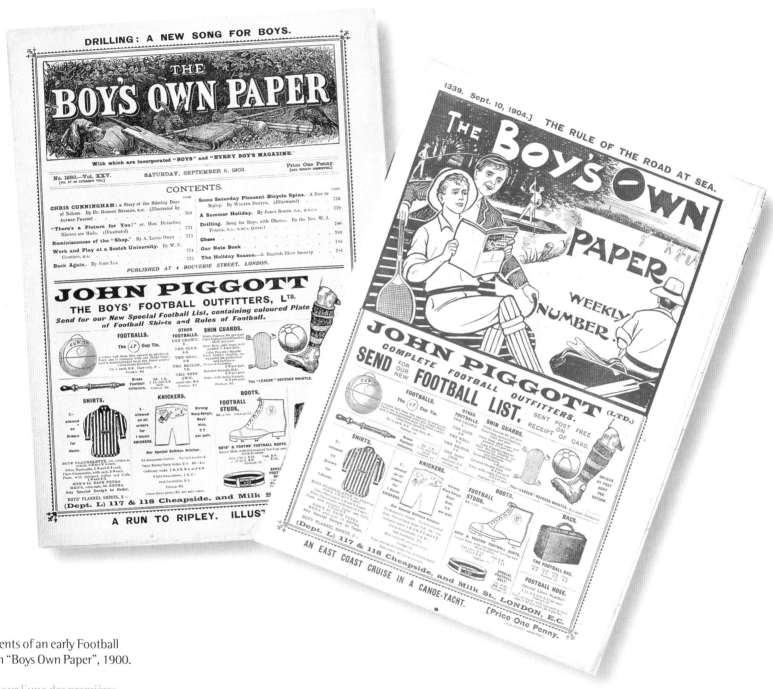

Advertisements of an early Football
Outfitters in "Boys Own Paper", 1900.

*Publicités pour l'une des premières
firmes de vêtements de football extrait
de «Boys Own Paper», 1900.*

Publicidad de un antiguo proveedor
futbolístico en "Boys Own Paper" 1900.

*Frühe Anzeige einer Ausrüstungsfirma
in „Boys Own Paper", 1900.*

Knitted woolen Soccer jerseys, 1880s style.

Maillot tricoté en laine, style des années 1880.

Jerseys de fútbol de lana tejido en el estilo de los años 80 del siglo XIX.

Wollene Strickjerseys im Stil von 1880/90.

Two shirts from 1910 and 1912 of the great Sheffield clubs (rivals then and now) – Wednesday on the left; United on the right.

Deux chemises de 1910 et 1912 des deux grands clubs de Sheffield (des riveaux alors et aujourd'hui) – Wednesday (à gauche) et United.

Dos camisas de 1910 y 1912 de los dos grandes clubes de Sheffield (rivales entonces y hoy) – Wednesday (izquierda) y United.

Zwei Hemden von 1910 und 1912 der beiden großen Klubs von Sheffield (Rivalen damals und heute) – Wednesday (links) und United.

Newcastle United FA Cup Final special jersey, 1907 (left) and a 1920s Australia shirt (right).

Maillot de Newcastle United pour la finale du FA Cup 1907 (à gauche) et une chemise australienne des années 1920.

Jersey de Newcastle United para la final del FA Cup de 1907 (izquierda), y una camisa australiana de los años 20.

Jersey von Newcastle United für das Endspiel des FA Cups 1907 (links) und ein australisches Hemd aus den zwanziger Jahren.

Two Soccer jerseys and a shirt, 1930s.

Deux maillots de Soccer et une chemise,
1930.

Dos jerseys de fútbol y una camisa,
años 30.

Zwei Jerseys und ein Hemd aus den
dreißiger Jahren.

Two pair of long woolen socks.   Deux paires de chaussettes montantes en laine.   Dos pares de calcetines largos de lana.   Zwei Paar lange Wollstrümpfe.

Blue Scottish Jersey (England vs. Scotland 1910) and the red England shirt with international badge, as worn by team in World Cup final vs. West Germany at Wembley, 1966.

Maillot écossais bleu (Angleterre contre Ecosse 1910) et chemise rouge de l'équipe d'Angleterre avec un badge international, qu'elle porta également lors de la finale de la Coupe du Monde contre L'Allemagne de l'Ouest à Wembley, 1966.

Jersey azul escocés (Inglaterra contra Escocia 1910) y la camisa roja inglesa con insignia internacional como la llevaba el equipo en la final del campeonato mundial contra Alemania Occidental en Wembley 1966.

Blaues schottisches Jersey vom Länderspiel England – Schottland 1910, und das rote England-Hemd mit internationalem Emblem, getragen 1966 beim Weltmeisterschafts-Endspiel gegen Westdeutschland im Wembley-Stadion.

Two pairs of brown Gentlemen's boots by Lillywhites, 1890s, of the type worn by the "Corinthian" footballers.

Deux paires de bottines pour hommes marons de chez Lillywhites, 1890 du même type que celles portée par les joueurs les «Corinthian».

Dos pares de botas marrones para caballeros de Lillywhites del mismo tipo que llevaban "Los Corintios", años 90 del siglo XIX.

Zwei Paar braune Herrenschuhe Marke Lillywhites, wie sie auch die Spieler der „Corinthians" um 1895 trugen.

The Cup-tie Football boots, 1900.

Bottines de football de la Coupe, 1900.

Las botas de fútbol del partido de copa 1900.

Fußballschuhe Marke „Cup-tie", 1900.

Pair of "Cup Final" boots with wicker-work pattern stamped on toes, 1910.

Paire de bottines très saillantes, spécialement conçues pour la finale de la Coupe avec «Pattern», 1910.

Un par de botas de la final de copa con dibujos enrejados estampados en las puntas, 1910.

Ein Paar „Cup Final" Schuhe von 1910, mit eingeprägtem Flechtwerkmuster.

Pair of children's boots,
size 7, 1920s.

Paire de bottines pour enfant,
taille 7, 1920.

Un par de botas para niños
número 7 de los años 20.

Kinderschuhe Größe 7,
zwanziger Jahre.

Examples of special boots, on the right side a pair of 1930s with unusual studs – now illegal.

Exemple de bottines spéciales, à droite une paire des années 1930 aux crampons inhabituels, aujourd'hui interdits.

Ejemplos de botas especiales, a la derecha un par de los años 30 con tacos anormales - hoy en día prohibidos.

Beispiele besonderer Schuhe, rechts ein Paar von 1930 mit ungewöhnlichen Stollen – heute nicht mehr erlaubt.

Orange colored ball of the 1880s, stuffed as medicine ball but classic shape.

Ballon colorée en orange des années 1880 de forme normale mais lestée comme un «medecine ball».

Balón pintado de naranja de los años 80 del siglo XIX en forma de un balón de medicina.

Orangefarbener Ball um 1885, gefertigt wie ein Medizinball, doch in der Größe eines Fußballs.

Soccer ball from the 1910s.

Ballon de football de 1910.

Balón de los años 10.

Fußball um 1910.

Pamphlets and a product from the British ball factory Duke & Son, early 20th century.

Pamphlets et produit de l'usine britannique de ballons Duke&Son, début du 20ème siècle.

Folletos y un producto de la fábrica británica de balones Duke & Son, principios del siglo XX.

Werbebroschüren und ein Ball der britischen Firma Duke & Son, Anfang 20. Jahrhundert.

Soccer balls 1900-1920.　　Ballons de Soccer 1900-1920.　　Balones 1900-1920.　　Fußbälle der Jahre 1900 bis 1920.

"Nesthill" brass Football pump, English 1890s, and an early 20th century pump.

Pompe à air «Nesthill» en airain, Angleterre 1890; et une pompe du début du 20ème siècle.

Bomba inglesa de latón "Nesthill", años 90 del siglo XIX y una bomba de principios del siglo XX.

Englische Messing-Fußballpumpe Marke „Nesthill", ca. 1895, und eine Pumpe vom Beginn des 20. Jahrhunderts.

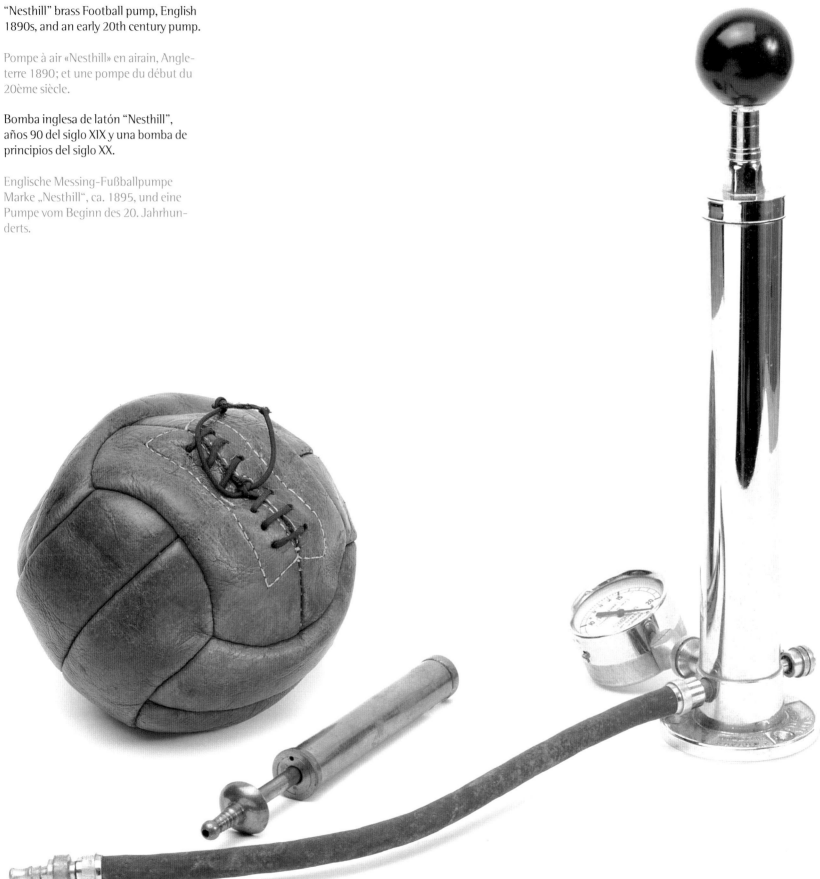

Four 1930 footballs in different colours as used in the 20th century in Florence for the revived game of "Il Calcio".

Quatre ballons de football de couleurs différentes de 1930, utilisés habituellement au 20ème siècle à Florence pour rappeler le jeu du «Il Calcio».

Cuatro balones de 1930 en varios colores como se usaban en el siglo XX en Florencia para el juego recuperado "Il Calcio".

Vier verschiedenfarbige Fußbälle von 1930, wie sie in Florenz für das wiederbelebte Spiel „Il Calcio" verwendet wurden.

Detail from a leather Soccer ball manufactured in the 1940s.

Détail d'un ballon de Soccer manufacturé dans les années 1940.

Detalle de un balón de cuero hecho en los años 40.

Detail eines Lederballs aus den vierziger Jahren.

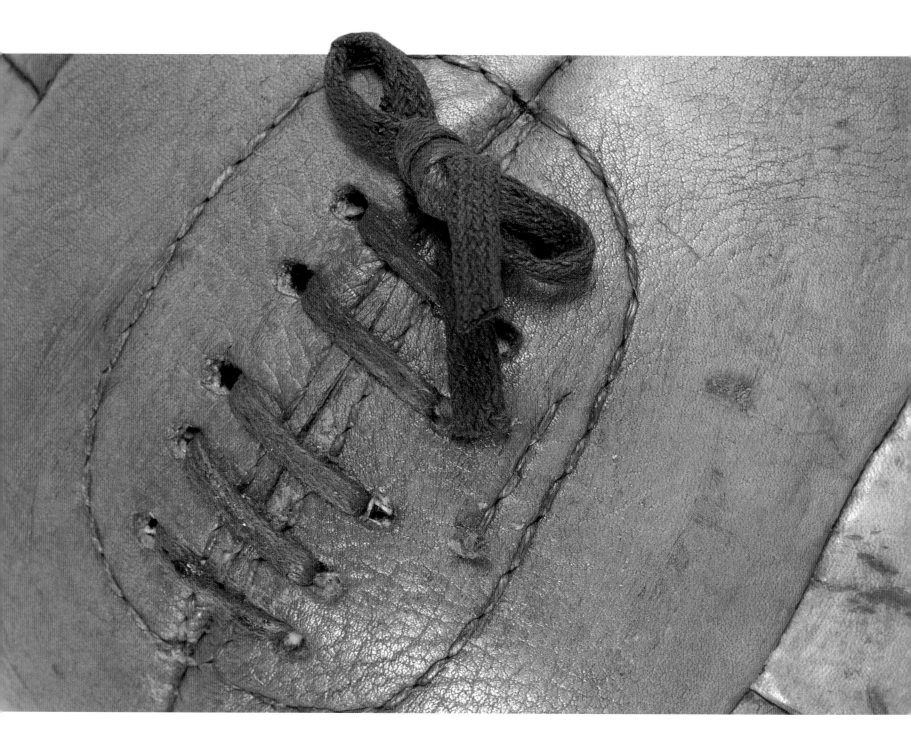

Modern Soccer ball of the 1960s.

Ballon moderne de 1960s.

Balón moderno de los 60.

Moderner Fußball der sechziger Jahre.

Long shinpads for use outside socks, 1890s.

De longs protèges tibias à porter sur les chaussettes, 1890.

Espinilleras largas para usar fuera de los calcetines, años 90 del siglo XIX.

Lange Schienbeinschützer, zu tragen über den Strümpfen, ca. 1895.

The short shinpads (in front) were used under socks, 1930s.

Les protèges tibias courts (sur le devant) étaient portés sous les chaussettes, 1930.

Espinilleras cortas (delante) eran usadas debajo de los calcetines, años 30.

Die kurzen Schienbeinschützer von 1930 (vorn) trug man unter den Strümpfen.

This German football game („Spiele, Heimchen, Spiele!") shows the use of the shinpads, early 20th century.

Ce tableau représentant un jeu allemand et où est inscrit («Spiele, Heimchen, Spiele!») illustre l'utilisation des protèges tibias au début du 20ème siècle.

Esta tapa de un juego alemán („Spiele, Heimchen, Spiele!") muestra el uso de las espinilleras, principios del siglo XX.

Dieses Fußballspiel aus Deutschland („Spiele, Heimchen, Spiele!"– Anfang 20. Jahrhundert) zeigt den Gebrauch der Schienbeinschützer.

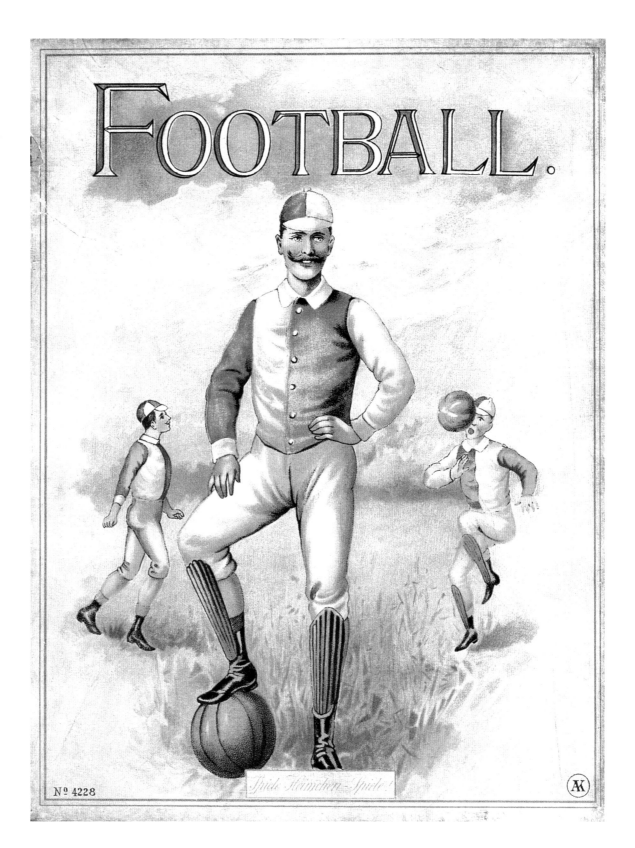

Historic boots, ball and shinpads – a collage.

Bottines historiques, ballon et protèges tibias - collage.

Botas históricas, balón y espinilleras - un montaje.

Historische Fußballschuhe, Ball und Schienbeinschützer – eine Collage.

Trainers bag. Leather "Gladstone" bag stamped with Ramsgate F. C. as used by trainers early 20th century. Contains old bottles of type used for embrocations and smelling salts.

Sac en cuir pour entraîneur, avec inscription du club Ramsgate F. C., début du 20ème siècle. Contenant entre autres des flacons avec des pommades pour friction et sels.

Maletín de cuero para entrenadores, con estampado Ramsgate F. C., principios del siglo XX. Contenía entre otras cosas pequeñas botellas con linimentos y sales volátiles.

Trainer-Tasche aus Leder, mit Klubprägung Ramsgate F.C., Anfang 20. Jahrhundert. Zum Inhalt gehörten u. a. Fläschchen mit Einreibungsmitteln und Riechsalz.

10 Art and Football
L'art et le football
Arte y fútbol
Kunst und Fußball

Art, they say, is where you see it. On the Football pitch, most supporters would wish. The visual arts sourrounding Football games are often plain and primitive if the artists have been honest. Such simplicity is like a direct shot or a simple pass: not to be despised. The blending of Art and Industry seemed as ludicrous to the 19th century Victorians as the notion of Art and Football remains to many lofty pundits even today. This chapter collects representative examples from the 19th century to the modern times: stoneware and porcelain, paintings and prints, posters, metallic art and sculptures, all using and presenting Football motifs and thus following the great boom of the period.

L'art, dit-on, est où vous le voyez. La plupart des supporters voudraient le trouver sur le terrain. Si les artistes étaient honnêtes, l'art relatif au football serait souvent simple et primitif. Cette simplicité c'est par exemple un tir direct ou une passe simple: on ne doit pas la mépriser. L'association de l'art et de l'industrie semblait aussi incongrue au 19 ème siècle à l'ère Victorienne, que celle des notions de football et d'art pour de nombreux grands experts contemporains. Cette partie de la collection contient des œuvres représentatives du 19 ème siècle à nos jours: poteries et porcelaines, peintures et reproductions, posters, objets métalliques et sculptures, tous ces objets s'inspirèrent et illustrèrent le football surtout durant sa période d'expansion.

El arte, como se dice, está en donde uno lo ve. En el campo de fútbol, la mayoría de los hinchas lo quisiera ver así. Las artes visuales que se inspiran en los juegos de fútbol son a menudo muy simples y prosaicas, si es que los artistas han sido honestos. Esta simplicidad es como un remate oportuno o un pase sencillo: no es de despreciar. La mezcla entre arte e industria parecía tan grotesca a la sociedad victoriana del siglo XIX, como la idea de arte y fútbol lo es aún hoy para muchos "expertos". En lo siguiente se encuentran ejemplos representativos desde el siglo XIX hasta los tiempos modernos: objetos de piedra y porcelana, pinturas y grabados, carteles, arte en metal y esculturas; utilizando y presentando motivos futbolísticos, acordes con la moda de la época.

Kunst, so heißt es, ist dort, wo man sie sieht. Das wünschten sich die meisten Fußballbegeisterten wohl auch. Doch die Kunstobjekte in Verbindung mit dem Spiel sind oft nüchtern und prosaisch, wenn die Künstler ehrlich waren. Solcher Purismus ist dem direkten Schuß oder einem einfachen Paß vergleichbar und also nicht geringzuschätzen. Den britischen Victorianern des 19. Jahrhunderts erschien freilich die Verbindung von Kunst und Industrie als ein ebenso zu belächelndes Phänomen wie es die Vorstellung einer Verbindung von Kunst und Fußball bis heute für viele hochmütige „Kenner" geblieben ist. Nachfolgend werden repräsentative Beispiele vom 19. Jahrhundert bis in die moderne Zeit vorgestellt: Stücke aus Keramik und Porzellan, Gemälde und Graphiken, Plakate sowie Skulpturen – allesamt unter Verwendung von Fußball-Motiven und damit dem großen Boom ihrer Zeit folgend.

From Doulton Lambeth: a two-handled tyg and two jugs from 1883/84. A fine and rare model of Soccer ball match holder with silver rim, from 1885 (right page, top).

Doulton Lambeth: Une cruche à deux poignées et deux pichets de 1883/84. Un modèle rare et raffiné de ballon de football, boîte d´allumette en argent de 1885 (en haut à droit).

De Doulton Lambeth: Una jarra y dos jarros de 1883/84. Un modelo elegante y singular de un balón, soporte de fósforos, con borde de plata de 1885 (arriba a la derecha).

Stücke aus Doulton Lambeth: eine zweihenklige Tasse und zwei Krüge von 1883/84. Ein seltener Streichholzhalter in Form eines Fußballs, 1885 (rechte Seite, oben).

Child's porcelain dish in metal hot water heater. East European, circa 1905.

Assiette pour enfant dans une cuvette chauffe-plats. Europe de l'Este, vers 1905.

Plato para niños en fuente metálica para mantenerlo caliente. Europa del Este, hacia 1905.

Kinderteller in metallenem Warmhaltebecken. Osteuropa um 1905.

Parian figures of Rugby schoolboy
and girl companion (left side) and a
Staffordshire figure of Rugby schoolboy, 1860s.

Figurines en parian représentant des
écoliers jouant au rugby accompagnés
de leurs admiratrices (côté gauche),
ainsi qu'une figurine du Staffordshire,
années 1860.

Figuras de un alumno de Rugby en
compañía de una muchacha (a la
izquierda) y una figura Staffordshire
de un alumno de Rugby de los años
60 del siglo XIX.

Keramikfiguren eines Rugby-Schulboys
und Schulmädchens (links) und die
Staffordshire-Figur eines Rugby-
Jungen, um 1865.

Staffordshire mugs, 1860s to 1880s. Tasses du Staffordshire, années de 1860 à 1880. Tazas de Staffordshire, entre los años 60 y 80 del siglo XIX. Tassen aus Staffordshire, 1860 bis 1880.

English glass flower vase, 1910, and a French vase from the same time.

Vase de verre anglais datant de 1910 et un vase français de la même époque.

Florero inglés de cristal 1910 y un florero francés de la misma época.

Englische und französische Vase, beide von 1910.

German beer stein, early 20th century. The inscription says: "O wonderful football game – the finest game of youth".

Chope de bière allemande du début du siècle. L'inscription dit : «Oh merveilleux football – le meilleur sport pour la jeunesse».

Jarra de cerveza alemana de principios del siglo XX. La inscripción dice: "Oh maravilloso fútbol – el mejor juego de la juventud".

Deutscher Bierkrug, Anfang 20. Jahrhundert. Die Inschrift lautet: „O wunderbares Fußballspiel – du schönstes Spiel der Jugend".

Copeland blue and white England
Football jug and cup, 1893, and a large
Belleek jug on American Football
(right).

Pichet et gobelet anglaises bleus et
blancs de Copeland, 1893, et une grande jarre Belleek avec une scène du Football Américain (à droite).

Jarra y vaso de fútbol ingleses, azules y
blancos de Copeland, 1893, y una jarra
grande Belleek con una escena del Fútbol Americano (derecha).

Blauweißer englischer Fußball-Krug
und -Becher von Copeland, 1893, und
ein großer Belleek-Krug mit einer Szene
vom American Football (rechts).

Ceramic armorial and miniature souvenirs from the early 20th century.

Céramiques armoriales et souvenirs miniatures du début du siècle.

Recuerdos de cerámica en forma de miniaturas de principios del siglo XX.

Keramik-Souvenirs vom Anfang der zwanziger Jahre.

Porcelain figures from famous
manufacturers: Kerbena, early 1930s,
and Wedgewood (left).

Personnages en porcelaine de
manufacturiers célèbres tels Kerbena
au début des annés 1930, et Wedgewood (à gauche).

Figuras de porcelana de manufacturas
famosas: Kerbena, hacia los años 30 y
Wedgewood (a la izquierda).

Porzellanfiguren aus berühmten
Manufakturen: Kerbena, Anfang der
dreißiger Jahre, und Wedgewood
(links).

Staffordshire sugar bowl, 1880s;
a Dan Doyle/W. J. Bassett
commemorative piece from the 1890s
and an 1896 FA Cup winners jug
(from left).

Sucrier Staffordshire des années 1880,
un pièce commémorative de
Dan Doyle / W.J. Bassett des années
1890 et un pichet du FA Cup de 1896
(en partant de la gauche).

Azucarero Staffordshire, años 80,
recuerdo Dan Doyle/W. J. Bassett de los
años 90 del siglo XIX y jarro del FA Cup
1896 (de la izquierda).

Staffordshire-Zuckerschale, um 1885;
ein Erinnerungsstück von
Dan Doyle/W. J. Bassett, um 1895, und
ein Krug mit dem Gewinner des FA-
Cups 1896 (von links).

Decorative ceramic pieces, late 1880s and early 1900s.

Objets décoratifs en céramiques, final des années 1880 et début du 20ème siècle.

Piezas decorativas de cerámica del final de los años 1880 y principios del siglo XX.

Dekorative Keramikstücke, Ende 19. und Anfang 20. Jahrhundert.

A pastiche of 14th Century football in London painted in the 20th century (acrylic on paper on board by "Farley"); the detail has been imagined from written descriptions of the period.

Pastiche d'un jeu de football londonien du 14ème siècle réalisé au 20ème siècle par «Farley»; le détail a été imaginé d'après des descriptions manuscrites de l'époque.

Pastiche del fútbol del siglo XIV, Londres, pintado en el siglo XX (acrílico sobre papel y tabla de "Farley"); los detalles se imaginaron según descripciones escritas de aquella época.

Fußball im London des 14. Jahrhunderts, gemalt im 20. Jahrhundert von „Farley". Die Details entnahm der Künstler alten Beschreibungen des Spiels.

"Old English scene" by Edward Lancaster, oils on canvas 1950. The typical village soccer match is included as a natural ingredient of English life.

«Vieille scène anglaise» d'Edward Lancaster, huile sur canevas 1950. Le match typique de football de village fait partie intégrante de la vie anglaise.

"Escena antigua inglesa" de Edward Lancaster, oleo sobre tela 1950. El típico partido del pueblo está incluido como un ingrediente natural de la vida inglesa.

„Alte englische Szenerie". Gemälde von Edward Lancaster, 1950. Das typische dörfliche Fußballspiel erscheint als natürlicher Bestandteil des Lebens in England.

The Football game in two English lithographs from the 19th century.

Le football représenté sur deux lithographies anglaises du 19ème siècle.

El fútbol en dos litografías inglesas del siglo XIX.

Fußballspiel in zwei englischen Lithographien aus dem 19. Jahrhundert.

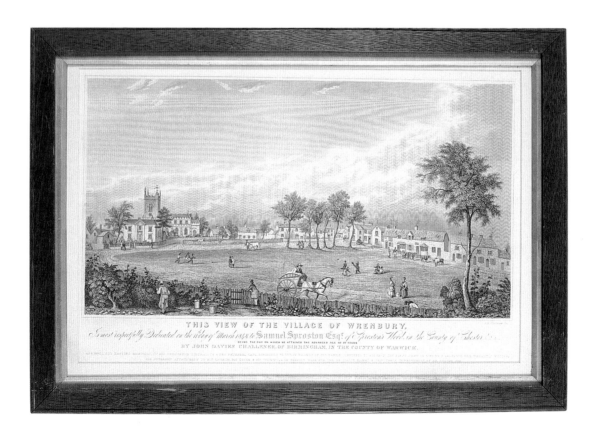

Great Dean's Yard. Boys playing football at Westminster School, London, in Mid-19th century. Lithograph from drawing by C. W. Radclyffe.

Garçons jouant au football dans le jardin de la Westminster School Londres, milieu du 19ème siècle. Lithografie d'aprés un dessin de C. W. Radclyffe.

Niños jugando al fútbol en el jardín de la Westminster School en Londres, mediados del siglo XIX. Litografía según un dibujo de C. W. Radclyffe.

Jungen beim Fußballspiel im Garten der Londoner Westminster School, Mitte 19. Jahrhundert. Lithographie nach einer Zeichnung von C. W. Radclyffe.

"Soccer match" by Gaston Vaudou, oils on canvas 1920.

«Match de Soccer» par Gaston Vaudou, huile sur canevas 1920.

"Partido de fútbol" de Gaston Vaudou, oleo sobre tela 1920.

„Fußball-Match". Gemälde von Gaston Vaudou, 1920.

"Football match at Chelsea" by
Mary Krishna, oils on canvas 1950s.

«Match de football à Chelsea» par
Mary Krishna, huile sur canevas 1950.

"Partido de fútbol en Chelsea" de
Mary Krishna, oleo sobre tela años 50.

„Fußball-Match in Chelsea". Gemälde
von Mary Krishna, ca. 1955.

"Study of Textures" by V. Coverly Price, oil painting 1960.

«Etude de texture» par V. Coverly Price, peinture à l'huile 1960.

"Estudio de estructuras" de V. Coverly Price, pintura en oleo 1960.

„Stilleben mit Bällen". Gemälde von V. Coverly Price, 1960.

"They were Christophers" by Doris Brand, oil painting 1950s.

«They were Christophers» par Doris Brand, peinture à l'huile 1950.

"Ellos eran Cristoferos" de Doris Brand, pintura en oleo años 50.

„Sie gehörten Christopher". Gemälde von Doris Brand, ca. 1955.

"In the Dressing room" , signed GOM, oils on board 1950s.

«Dans les vestiaires» signé GOM, huile sur planche 1950.

"En la cabina", firmado GOM, oleo sobre tabla años 50.

„Im Umkleideraum". Gemälde von GOM, ca. 1955.

"Les Footballeurs" by Jean Oliver, 1974.

«Les footballeurs» par Jean Oliver, 1974.

"Les Footballeurs" de Jean Olivier, 1974.

„Die Fußballer". Gemälde von Jean Olivier, 1974.

"Maradona Goal" by Chris Holwell,
acrylic on upholstered canvas, 1970s.

«But de Madona» par Chris Holwell,
acrylique sur canevas, 1970.

"Gol de Maradona" de Chris Holwell,
acrílico sobre tela tapizada, años 70.

„Tor durch Maradona". Acryl auf gepol-
stertem Grund von Chris Holwell,
ca. 1975.

African batik picture from Uganda,
illustrating Football in modern times.

Batik africain d´Ouganda illustrant le
football d´aujourd´hui.

Imagen teñida africana de Uganda
ilustrando fútbol en la época moderna.

Diese afrikanische Batikarbeit aus
Uganda zeigt den modernen Fußball.

"The Game of the Year" by Ithell
Colquhoun, oils on canvas, 1953.

«Le jeu de l´année» par Ithell
Colquhoun, huile sur canevas, 1953.

"El partido del año" de Ithell
Colquhoun, oleo sobre tela 1953.

„Spiel des Jahres". Gemälde von
Ithell Colquhoun, 1953.

"Football at Rio de Janeiro" by S. Brandão, mixed media painting on canvas, 1960s.

«Football à Rio de Janeiro» par S. Brandão, peintures mélangées sur canevas, 1960.

"Fútbol en Río de Janeiro" de S. Brandão, pintura de técnicas mixtas sobre tela, años 60.

„Fußball in Rio de Janeiro". Gemälde von S. Brandão, ca. 1965.

Peruvian fabric collage of a Football match, 1970s.

Collage péruvien d´un match de football, années 1970.

Montaje del Perú de un partido de fútbol, años 70.

Collage aus Peru, ca. 1975.

Oxford vs. Cambridge. Print of a match at Queen's Club, early 1900s.

Rencontre Oxford – Cambridge au Queen's Club. Impression vers 1905.

Partido Oxford – Cambridge en el Queen's Club. Estampa hacia 1905.

Begegnung Oxford – Cambridge im Queen's Club. Druck um 1905.

Spanish poster, published Valencia early
20th century.

Affiche espagnole de Valencia, début
du 20ème siècle.

Cartel español de Valencia, principios
del siglo XX.

Spanisches Plakat aus Valencia,
Anfang 20. Jahrhundert.

Two Art Deco-ish designs for transport poster, possibly London Underground. Signed B. P., mid-20th century.

Deux exemples art-déco certainement issus de l'Underground londonien signé B. P., milieu du 20ème siècle.

Dos diseños de estilo Art Deco para avisos de transporte, posiblemente del metro de Londres. Firmado B. P., mediados del siglo XX.

Zwei Plakatentwürfe im Stil der zwanziger Jahre, wahrscheinlich für die Londoner Untergrundbahn, um 1950.

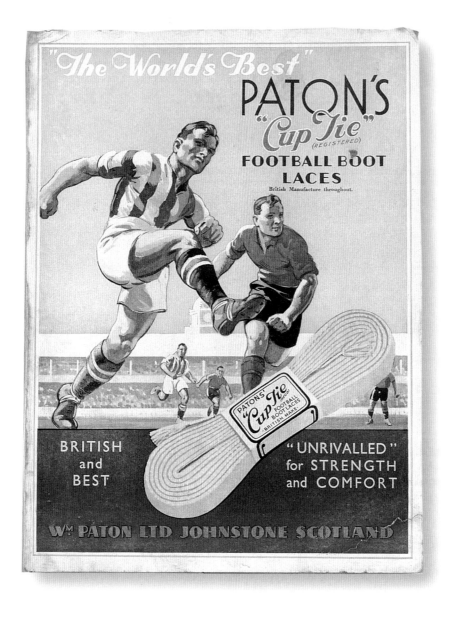

Paton's Cup-tie football bootlaces advertising card, 1930s-50s.

Publicité pour les lacets de football de compétition Paton, 1930-50.

Tarjeta publicitaria para cordones de fútbol Cup-tie de Paton, años 30-50.

Werbekarte der Firma Paton für Fußballschnürsenkel, dreißiger bis fünfziger Jahre.

French poster from the late 1930s.

Poster français de la fin des années 1930.

Cartel francés de fin de los años 30.

Französisches Plakat, Ende der 30er Jahre.

Italian advertising card, 1920.

Publicité italienne, 1920.

Tarjeta de publicidad italiana, 1920.

Italienische Werbekarte, 1920.

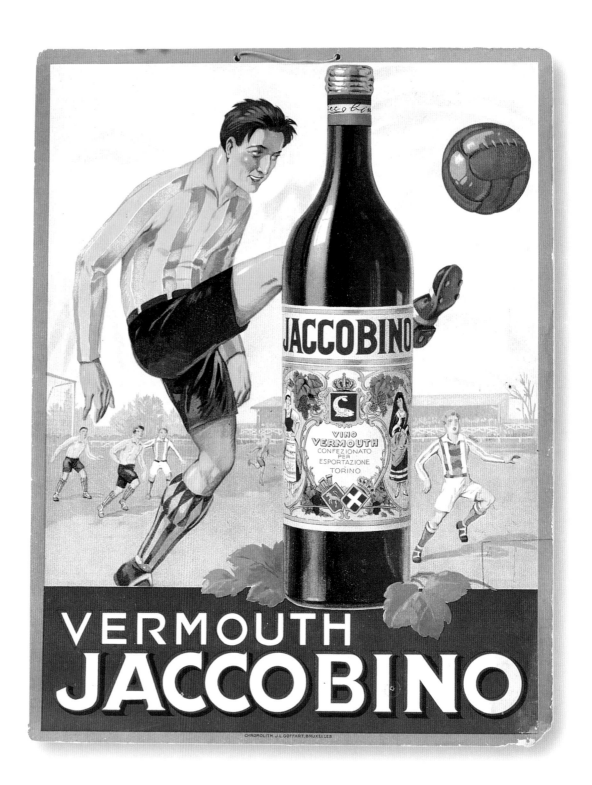

British World War II poster, using the Football game to stimulate the buying of National Savings.

Poster anglais de la deuxième guerre mondiale, utilisant le football comme stimulant pour la défense nationale.

Cartel británico de la segúnda guerra mundial usando el fútbol para estimular la compra de empréstitos nacionales.

Britisches Plakat aus dem Zweiten Weltkrieg. Fußball als Werbeanreiz zum Kauf von Kriegsanleihen.

English bronze, showing C. Wrenford
Brown of the Corinthians at the
thrown-in, 1890s.

Bronzes anglais montrant C. Wrenford
Brown des Corinthians réalisant une
touche, 1890.

Bronce inglés mostrando C. Wrenford
Brown de los Corintios sacando fuera de
banda, años 90 del siglo XIX.

Englische Bronzestatuette, ca. 1895.
Dargestellt ist C. Wrenford Brown von
den Corinthians beim Einwurf.

A pair of brass chimney ornaments,
molded "flats" with silhouettes of a
Rugby and Soccer player. These figures
were manufactured in Britain for a long
period starting around 1880.

Paire de bronze d'ornement de
cheminée représentant des silhouettes
de joueurs de football et de rugby. Ces
figures furent manufacturées en
Angleterre durant une longue période
qui débuta vers 1880.

Un par de ornamentos de latón para la
chimenea, representando siluetas de un
jugador de Rugby y un futbolista. Se
producían estas figuras en Gran Bretaña
durante largo tiempo empezando hacia
1880.

Kaminfiguren aus Bronze – ein Rugby-
und ein Fußballspieler. Solche Figuren
wurden ab 1880 in Großbritannien für
lange Zeit hergestellt.

Dutch or Belgian metal figures by
J. Lisse, 1910.

Figurines en métal belges ou
hollandaises par J. Lisse, 1910.

Figuras holandesas o belgas de metal de
J. Lisse, 1910.

Metallfiguren von J. Lisse (Holland oder
Belgien), 1910.

French spelter figure by Ruffony, 1930s.

Figurine française par Ruffony, 1930.

Figura francesa de cinc de Ruffony, años 30.

Französische Figur von Ruffony, ca. 1930.

Two Belgian spelter figures from the 1920s (player and goalkeeper). In the middle a French figure of 1910, the brass plaque inscribed "Challenge de l'Amitié Franco – Belge".

Deux personnages belges des années 1920 (joueur et gardien de but). Au milieu une figurine française de 1910, sur la plaque est inscrit «Challenge de l'Amitié Franco–Belge».

Dos figuras belgas de cinc de los años 20 (futbolista y portero). En el centro una figura francesa de 1910, en la placa de latón está escrito "Challenge de l'Amitié Franco–Belge".

Zwei belgische Figuren (Spieler und Torhüter) aus den zwanziger Jahren, in der Mitte eine französische Figur von 1910 mit Messingschild „Challenge de l'Amitié Franco–Belge".

Two French spelter figures from the
1920s.

Deux personnages françaises des
années 1920.

Dos figuras francesas de cinc de los
años 20.

Zwei französische Figuren aus den
zwanziger Jahren.

Silver-plated plaster group, English
1953.

Groupe de platre recouvert d'argent,
Angleterre 1953.

Grupo de yeso cubierto de plata,
Inglaterra 1953.

Versilberte Gips-Figurengruppe,
England, 1953.

11 Decorative Items
Les objets décoratifs
Objetos decorativos
Dekorative Stücke

Football players and their clubs, from the first, sought to enhance their triumphs with mementoes of the game. Medals, buttons, lockets, match holders, penknives, clocks and watches, and a multitude of other souvenirs, joined the obligatory medals and trophies. The bulk of the finer early material, from the 1870s to the start of the first world war in 1914, was made in and for Britain. Craftsmen like Vaughton's of Birmingham and Fattorini of Bradford produced tens of thousands of items in gold, silver, bronze and other metals. In an age newly conscious of fitness and exercise, women wore delicate Football lockets with their favorite man's likeness inside, perhaps opposite a lock of his hair. Such days, gentlemen. Such days!

This chapter presents a representative selection of the various kinds of items, from the exceptional to the "kitsch".

Les joueurs de football et leurs clubs cherchèrent dès le départ à associer à leurs victoires des objets commémoratifs. Aux incontournables médailles et trophées, se sont ajoutés des badges, des boutons, des médaillons, des boîtes d'allumettes, des stylos, des couteaux des pendules et des montres, ainsi qu'une multitude d'autres objets.

La majeure partie de ces objets raffinés fut fabriquée en Grande Bretagne pour des Anglais, des années 1870 au début de la première guerre mondiale en 1914. Des artisans tels Vaughton's de Birmingham et Fattorini de Bradford produisirent des dizaines de milliers d'objets en or, en argent, en bronze ou en d'autres métaux. A une époque, où l'on avait pris conscience depuis peu de la valeur de l'exercice physique, les femmes arboraient des pendentifs ayant pour thème le football avec le portrait de son amant d'un côté et une mèche de ses cheveux de l'autre côté. Quelle époque, Messieurs. Quelle époque!

Ce chapitre présente une sélection significative de ces objets, dont certains sont véritablement charmants, et d'autres vraiment «kitsch».

Clubes y jugadores de fútbol buscaron desde el principio perennizar sus triunfos con recuerdos del juego. Medallas, botones, medallones, cajas de cerillas, navajas, relojes y una gran variedad de otros recuerdos acompañaron a los trofeos obligatorios.

La mayor parte de estos objetos finos inicialmente usados, desde 1870, hasta el comienzo de la primera guerra mundial en 1914, fue confeccionada en y para Gran Bretaña. Artesanos como Vaughton`s de Birmingham y Fattorini de Bradford produjeron cientos de miles de artículos en oro, plata, bronce y otros metales. Cuando se tomó conciencia del valor del buen estado físico y de los ejercicios, muchas mujeres empezaron a llevar medallones de fútbol que contenían en su interior la foto de su amado y en el otro lado quizás un mechón de su cabello. ¡Qué tiempos, señores! ¡Qué tiempos!

En este capítulo se encuentra una selección representativa de los diferentes tipos de artículos, algunos de ellos realmente bonitos y algunos realmente cursis.

Von Anfang an trachteten die Fußballheroen und ihre Klubs danach, ihre Triumphe mit Erinnerungsstücken zu verewigen. So entstanden neben den obligatorischen Sieger-Medaillen und Trophäen auch Anstecker, Medaillons, Aufnäher, Taschenmesser, Tisch- und Taschenuhren sowie eine Vielzahl weiterer Fußballsouvenirs – die Mehrzahl der frühen Stücke von 1870 bis zum Beginn des Ersten Weltkriegs 1914 in und für Großbritannien. Kunsthandwerkliche Betriebe wie Vaughton's in Birmingham und Fattorini in Bradford produzierten zehntausende Exemplare in Gold, Silber, Bronze und anderen Metallen. In einem Zeitalter neu erwachten sportlichen Bewußtseins trugen die Frauen feinste Fußball-Medaillons mit den Porträts ihrer Auserwählten, oft kombiniert mit einer Haarlocke. Das waren Zeiten, meine Herren! Das waren Zeiten! Nachfolgend eine repräsentative Auswahl dieser verschiedenen Memorabilia, von außergewöhnlichen Stücken bis hin zu Kitsch.

Two decorative brass clocks, English, made between 1880 and 1890, each with a Soccer scene.

Deux pendules décoratives en étain anglaises réalisées entre 1880 et 1890, représentant chacune une scène de football.

Dos relojes decorativos ingleses de latón, hechos entre 1880 y 1890, cada uno decorado con una escena de fútbol.

Zwei dekorative britische Tischuhren aus Messing mit Fußballszenen, nach 1880.

Enameled metal traveling clock in the shape of 1930s soccer ball and two small white metal table-knife rests from the 1890s.

Réveil de métal emaillé en forme de ballon de football des années 1930, et deux fins couteaux de table en métal blanc des années 1890.

Reloj de viaje de metal esmaltado en forma de un balón de los años 30 y dos pequeños soportes de metal para cuchillos, hechos en los años 90 del siglo XIX.

Reiseuhr in Form eines Fußballs, um 1930, und zwei kleine Messerablagen von 1890.

Two decorative Swiss made pocket watches from the 1910s, a Birmingham silver cigarette case from 1903 and two British silver Vestas (one in the shape of a soccer ball) from the 1900s.

Deux montres suisses ornementées de 1910, un étui à cigarettes en argent de Birmingham de 1903 et deux Vestas britanniques en argent, dont l'une en forme de ballon de football, des années 1900.

Dos relojes decorativos de bolsillo hechos en Suiza en los años 10, una pitillera de plata de Birmingham de 1903 y dos porta-cerillas británicos (uno en forma de un balón) de principios del siglo XX.

Zwei Schweizer Taschenuhren (um 1910), ein silbernes Zigarettenetui aus Birmingham (1903) sowie zwei silberne britische Streichholzschachtelhüllen (nach 1900).

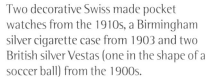

Some examples of silver and brass Vestas, early 20th century.

Quelques exemples de Vestas en argent et en étain, début du 20ème siècle.

Unos ejemplos de portacerillas de plata y latón, principios del siglo XX.

Beispiele für Streichholzschachtelhüllen aus Silber und Messing, Anfang 20. Jahrhundert.

German wooden cuckoo clock with moving figures, probably made as a souvenir of the 1936 Olympics.

Horloge à coucou en bois d´Allemagne avec des personnages animés, probablement en souvenir des Jeux Olympiques de 1936.

Reloj de cuco alemán con figuras móviles, probablemente hecho como recuerdo de los Juegos Olímpicos de 1936.

Deutsche Kuckucksuhr mit beweglichen Figuren, hergestellt wahrscheinlich als Souvenir für die Olympiade von 1936.

Black British cigarette case from the 1880s and an Austrian or Hungarian fine enameled piece, 1920s. Below an English folded hairbrush from the 1900s.

Etui noir à cigarettes anglais des années 1880 et pièce émaillée d'Autriche ou de Hongrie recouvertes de fins motifs, des années 1920. En bas, brosse à cheveux anglaise du début du siècle.

Pitillera británica en color negro de los años 80 del siglo XIX y una pieza esmaltada austríaca o húngara de los años 20. Debajo un cepillo de cabeza doblado de principios del siglo XX.

Schwarzes britisches Zigarettenetui (um 1880), österreich-ungarisches emailliertes Etui (ca. 1925) sowie eine britische ausklappbare Haarbürste (um 1900).

Some silver and copper medals, two penknifes and a Vesta in shape of a woman football player's leg, all late 19th/early 20th century.

Médailles en argent et en cuivre, deux couteaux et une vesta en forme de jambe de joueuse de football de la fin du 19ème siècle et du début du 20ème.

Unas medallas de plata y cobre, dos cortaplumas y un portacerillas en forma de una pierna de una jugadora de fútbol, todo de fin del siglo XIX/principios del siglo XX.

Silber- und Kupfermedaillen, zwei Taschenmesser und eine Streichholz-schachtelhülle in Form des Beines einer Fußballspielerin, Ende 19./Anfang 20. Jahrhundert.

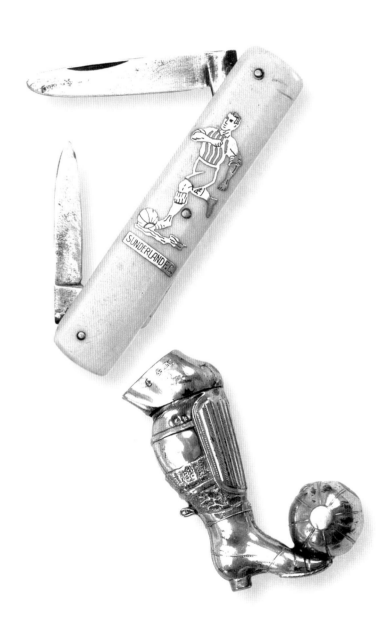

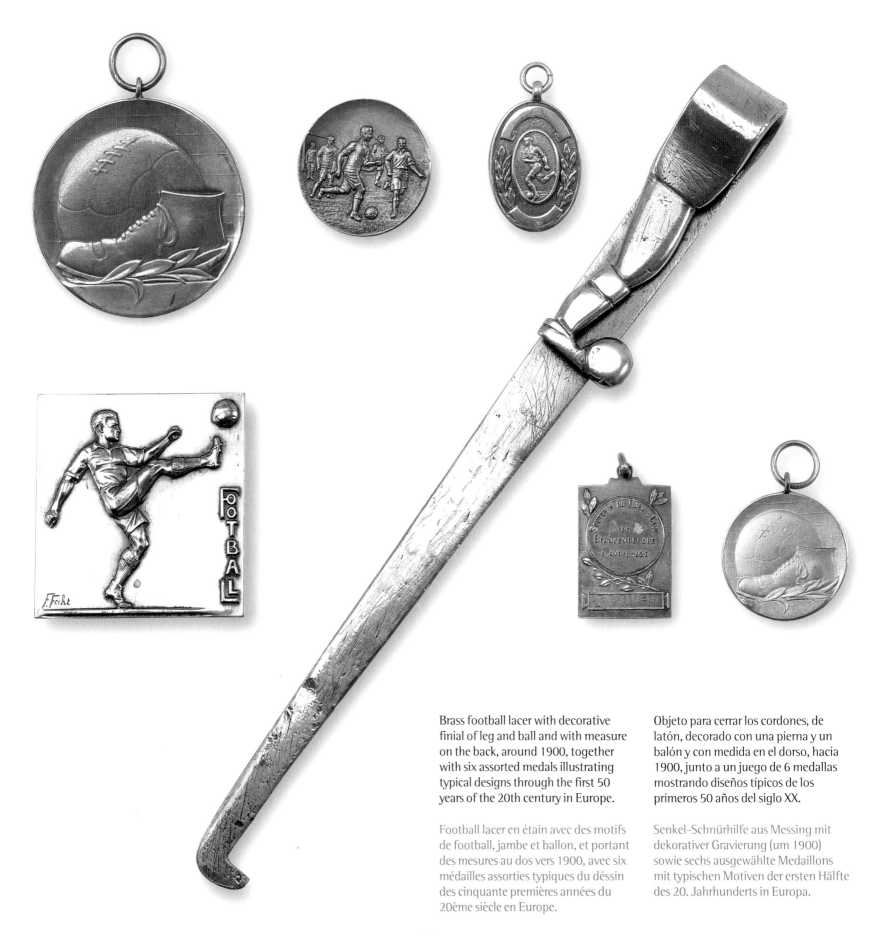

Brass football lacer with decorative finial of leg and ball and with measure on the back, around 1900, together with six assorted medals illustrating typical designs through the first 50 years of the 20th century in Europe.

Football lacer en étain avec des motifs de football, jambe et ballon, et portant des mesures au dos vers 1900, avec six médailles assorties typiques du déssin des cinquante premières années du 20ème siècle en Europe.

Objeto para cerrar los cordones, de latón, decorado con una pierna y un balón y con medida en el dorso, hacia 1900, junto a un juego de 6 medallas mostrando diseños típicos de los primeros 50 años del siglo XX.

Senkel-Schnürhilfe aus Messing mit dekorativer Gravierung (um 1900) sowie sechs ausgewählte Medaillons mit typischen Motiven der ersten Hälfte des 20. Jahrhunderts in Europa.

Silver ball from St. Columb, Cornwall, with stand. In the old Cornish language the inscription around the ball reads: "Fair play is good play". Beneath we see real "kitsch": a heavy ceramic inkwell in form of a Soccer ball and a sample of the different forms of souvenir pipes.

Balle en argent de St. Columb, Cornouaille, avec socle. Deux objets très «kitsch», une lourde bouteille d´encre en céramique en forme de ballon de football et une pipe en argile à embout en bambou.

Balón de plata de St. Columb, Cornwall, con soporte. Debajo vemos una auténtica cursilería: un tintero pesado de cerámica en forma de un balón y un ejemplo de las diferentes formas de pipas de recuerdo.

Silberner Ball mit Ständer aus St. Columb, Cornwall. Dazu echter Kitsch: Keramik-Tintenfaß in Form eines Fußballs und ein Beispiel für die Vielzahl von Souvenir-Tabakspfeifen.

Pictorial Dutch and British biscuit tins with printed decoration from the 1920s and 30s, the British piece with famous Blackburn Rovers players.

Boîtes à biscuits hollandaises ou anglaises décorée des années 1920 et 1930. Pièce anglaise représentant les fameux joueurs Blackburn Rovers.

Cajas pintorescas de hojalata para galletas de Holanda y Gran Bretaña con decoración imprimida de los años 20 y 30, la pieza británica con futbolistas famosos de los Blackburn Rovers.

Bedruckte holländische und britische Biskuitdosen aus den zwanziger und dreißiger Jahren. Das britische Exemplar zeigt berühmte Spieler der Blackburn Rovers.

Two more tins and a wooden pencil box with ornate transfer decoration on lid of an England vs Scotland match in 1897.

Deux boîtes métalliques et un coffret à stylos avec une décoration représentant l'Angleterre contre l'Ecosse en 1897.

Otras dos cajas de hojalata y un estuche de madera para lápices con decoración de calcomanía en la tapadera mostrando un partido de fútbol Inglaterra contra Escocia en 1897.

Zwei weitere Dosen und eine hölzerne Bleistift-Schachtel mit Abziehbild zur Erinnerung an das Länderspiel England – Schottland 1897.

French and British souvenir plates.

Plates commémoratives françaises et anglaises.

Platos de recuerdo franceses y británicos.

Französischer und britischer Wandteller.

Childrens money box and a child's
Football supporter rattle.

Tirelires d'enfants et fanion d'enfants
supporteurs de football.

Hucha infantil y una carraca de
aficionados al fútbol.

Sparbüchse und Rassel für Kinder.

Some examples of postcards from the 1920s and 30s.

Quelques exemples de cartes postales des annés 1920 et 1930.

Unos ejemplos de tarjetas postales de los años 20 y 30.

Postkarten aus den zwanziger und dreißiger Jahren.

Pair of decorative trays with enameled pictures of rugby and football on porcelain set into silver rings. Hallmarked Birmingham 1907.

Deux coupes décoratives en argent avec des scénes de rugby et de football sur le fond en porcelaine. Emprinted Birmingham 1907.

Dos fuentes decorativas de plata con escenas de rugby y fútbol en el fondo de porcelana. Sellado Birmingham 1907.

Zwei dekorative Silberschalen mit Rugby- und Fußballszenen auf dem Porzellanboden. Stempel Birmingham 1907.

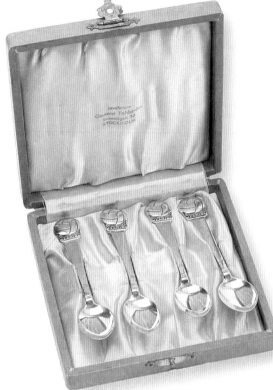

Set of four silver teaspoons in grey leatherette box with golden lettering "Skottland–Sveridge 1953".

Quatre cuilléres á thèe dans un étui en cuir avec inscription en or «Skottland–Sveridge 1953».

Cuatro cucharitas de plata en estuche de cuero con inscripción color de oro "Skottland–Sveridge 1953".

Vier silberne Teelöffel in Lederetui mit goldener Aufschrift „Skottland–Sveridge 1953".

"The Captain". Plaster figure by
E. Kinsella, 1907. Right side: 1890s
German bisque of boy and girl
footballers handcolored for Western
market.

«Le capitaine». Figure en plâtre par
E. Kinsella, 1907. A droite: Figurines
allemandes des années 1890 représentant des garçons et des filles jouant
au football colorées à la main pour le
marché de l'Ouest.

"El capitán". Figura de yeso de
E. Kinsella, 1907. A la derecha: grupo
de niños y niñas futbolistas de porcelana
coloreada a mano, para la exportación
al mercado de Europa del Oeste.
Alemania, años 90 del siglo XIX.

„Der Kapitän". Gipsfigur von
E. Kinsella, 1907. Rechte Seite: Hand-
bemalte Porzellanfiguren aus Deutschland für den Export nach Westeuropa,
ca. 1895.

— 251 —

Beer bottles with Football labels.

Bouteilles de bière avec des etiquettes de football.

Botellas de cerveza con rótulos de fútbol.

Bierflaschen mit Fußball-Etiketten.

Set of six vest buttons "L. and Co." English make, with photographic decorations in gold-plated holders.

Six vest buttons, Angleterre.

Juego de seis botones de chaleco ingleses "L. and Co." con decoraciones fotográficas en marcos cubiertos de oro.

Sechs britische Knöpfe (Firma „L. and Co.") mit Fotomotiven in Goldrahmen.

Umbrella stand made of cast iron, late 19th century.

Porte parapluie en fer, fin du 19ème siècle.

Soporte de paraguas hecho de hierro colado, fin del siglo XIX.

Gußeiserner Schirmständer, Ende 19. Jahrhundert.

"Fidelity" medal ribbon and three silver medals on chain plus flint lighter in the shape of a football boot.

Médaille «Fidelity» et trois médailles en argent pendant d'une chaîne et un briquet en forme d'une chaussure de football.

Medalla "Fidelity" y tres medallas de plata en una cadena al lado de un mechero en forma de una bota de fútbol.

Medaille „Fidelity" und drei silberne Medaillen an Kette, dazu ein Feuerzeug in Form eines Fußballschuhs.

Some examples of children's and armorial ceramic souvenirs, early 20th century.

Souvenirs pour la jeunesse, 1910.

Unos ejemplos de recuerdos para niños de cerámica, principios del siglo XX.

Beispiele von Keramiksouvenirs für Kinder, Anfang 20. Jahrhundert.

Silver plated decorative football trophy,
English 1870s.

Trophée de football recouverte
d´argent, Angleterre, années 1870.

Trofeo futbolístico decorativo cubierto
de plata, Inglés, años 70 del siglo XIX.

Dekorative versilberte Fußball-Trophäe,
England ca. 1870.

12 Toys and Games
Jeux et jouets
Jugetes y juegos
Spielzeug und Spiele

Football has inspired enthusiasts to play miniature games about the game for over a century. In recent years, video games imitating the real thing almost magically have sprouted world-wide. There is also the phenomenon of "fantasy football" where, informed almost hour by hour by telephonic and tele-video means, fanatical supporters can "play" each other at World Cup level even if they don't tackle their aged grandfather in real life. Toys and games from former times remain fascinating because often they present a more accurate and vivid picture of Football and its impact on billions of people than any other source of information. Miniature teams glow from their boxes, card games reveal ancient heroes, box tops record playing strips and stadiums long discarded. Last but not least: Looking at all these very decorative items creates a wonderful nostalgic emotion!

Depuis plus d'un siècle, le football inspire aux amoureux de ce sport, des jeux miniatures sur le football. Ces dernières années, les jeux vidéo imitant presque par magie la réalité, ont envahi le monde entier. Il existe aussi le phénomène des «jeux de football imaginaires» dans lesquels les supporters fanatiques, informés pratiquement d'heure en heure par téléphone ou par des moyens télévisuels, jouent ensemble au niveau de la Coupe du Monde, même s'ils n'oseraient pas affronter leur propre grand-père dans la réalité.
Les jouets et les jeux du passé demeurent fascinants, parce qu'ils offrent souvent une image plus précise et vivante du football et de son impact sur des milliards de personnes, que toute autre chose. Les équipes miniatures brillent au fond de leur boîte, les jeux de cartes nous rappellent les héros d'autrefois et les couvercles de boîte les équipes et les stades depuis longtemps oubliés. Enfin et surtout, regarder ces objets décoratifs nous remplit d'une douce nostalgie!

Por más de un siglo el fútbol ha entusiasmado a muchos a jugarlo en miniatura. En años recientes, los juegos de video, imitando casi mágicamente la realidad, se han difundido a lo largo y ancho del mundo. Tambien existe el fenómeno del "fantasy football", en el cual los fanáticos hinchas, informados casi hora por hora telefonicamente y por medios electrónicos, pueden "jugar" uno con otro al nivel de la Copa Mundial, aún cuando en la vida real ni se atreverían a desafiar a su abuelo. Jugetes y juegos de tiempos pasados todavía poseen una gran fascinación porque, representan una imagen más definida y viva del fútbol y su impacto en millones de personas que cualquier otra fuente de información. Equipos en miniatura brillan desde sus cajas, juegos de cartas muestran antiguos héroes, estuches recuerdan colores de equipos y estadios ya hace mucho tiempo fuera de servicio. Y así también, ¡el mirar todos estos objetos decorativos proporciona una hermosa emoción nostálgica!

Seit mehr als 100 Jahren hat der Fußball seine Fans dazu inspiriert, den Wettkampf mit Miniatur-Spielen nachzuvollziehen. In jüngster Zeit haben sich entsprechende Videospiele fast magisch weltweit ausgebreitet. Ebenso kann man das Phänomen des „Phantasie-Fußballs" beobachten, bei dem fanatische Fans mittels beinahe stündlicher Telefon- oder Internet-information gegeneinander auf Weltcupniveau „spielen" können – auch wenn sie im realen Leben niemals einen Fußball auch nur anrühren.
Spielzeug und Spiele aus vergangenen Jahren haben ihre Faszination behalten, weil sie oft ein genaueres und lebendigeres Bild vom Fußball und seiner Massenwirkung vermitteln als jede andere Informationsquelle. Aus den Schachteln blicken uns die Miniatur-Teams an, Kartenspiele erinnern an die Heroen von einst, die Hüllen zeigen längst verschwundene Stadien und Ausrüstungen.
Und nicht zu vergessen das herrlich nostalgische Gefühl beim Betrachten dieser Stücke!

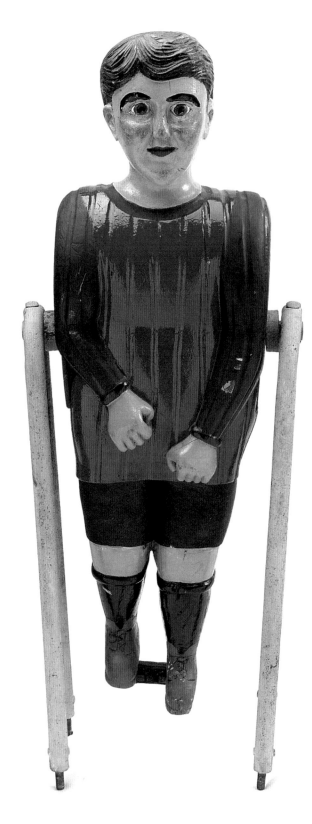

"The world's delight" – Wooden models of Soccer player plus stand from a Blackpool seaside arcade game, mid-1880s. Made in Naples.

Joueurs de football en bois et socles d'un jeu d'un salon de jeux de Blackpool, milieu des années 1880, fabriqués en Naples.

Modelos de madera de futbolistas y soportes de un juego de un salón de juegos de Blackpool, mediados de los años 80 del siglo XIX, fabricados en Nàpoles.

Drehbare Holzfiguren von einem Fußball-Spiel aus einer Spielhalle in Blackpool, ca. 1885, hergestellt in Neapel.

Smallest football game in matchbox,
probably Japanese, 1930s.

Jeu de football miniature dans une
boîte d'allumettes, probablement
japonais, 1930.

El futbolín más pequeño en una caja
de fósforos, probablemente japonés de
los años 30.

Das kleinste Fußballspiel in einer
Streichholzschachtel, dreißiger Jahre,
wahrscheinlich Japan.

"Penalty". Three metal figures, 1890,
the attackers with spring-loaded
kicking legs.

«Penalty». Trois figurines en métal,
1890, les attaquants avec des jambes
mouvantes au moyen de ressorts.

"Penalty". Tres figuras de metal, 1890,
los delanteros lanzan el balón por
medio de las piernas impulsadas de
muelles.

„Elfmeter". Drei Metallfiguren von
1890, die Schützen mit federndem
Spielbein.

A wooden articulated figure,
1900s.

Une personnage articulé en bois,
1900.

Una figura articulada de madera,
1900.

Bewegliche Holzfigur,
nach 1900.

Tin-plate clockwork figure with key. Made in "U. S. Zone Germany", 1950s.

Figurine à remonter en fer-blanc avec la clef, fabriquée en Allemagne à la zone occupée par les Etats Unis, années 1950.

Juguete de resorte de hojalata con la llave correspondiente, fabricado en Alemania en la parte ocupada por los E.E.U.U. en los años 50.

Aufziehbare Blech-Spielfigur mit dazugehörigem Schlüssel, hergestellt in den fünfziger Jahren in Deutschland, "U. S. Zone".

Blow Football, British, c1925.   Blow football, Angleterre, 1925.   Futbolín de soplar, Inglaterra, años 20.   Blas-Fußball, Großbritannien, ca. 1925.

Tommy Lawton jigsaw puzzle, late 1940s.

Puzzle de Tommy Lawton, fin des années 1940.

Rompecabezas de Tommy Lawton, fin de los años 40.

Puzzlespiel „Tommy Lawton", Ende vierziger Jahre.

"The Quick Change Artiste". Set of wooden play blocks in a box. British c1895.

«The Quick Change Artiste». Cubes en bois pour jeu. Angleterre, environ 1895.

"The Quick Change Artiste". Dados de madera. Inglaterra, hacia 1895.

„The Quick Change Artiste". Holz-Spielwürfel, England ca. 1895.

Snap. Card game, early 20th century.

Snap. Carte de football, du début du 20ème siècle.

Snap. Juego de cartas, principios del siglo XX.

Kartenspiel „Snap", Anfang 20. Jahrhundert.

Kick. A boxed game from the 1900s with eight mechanical figures plus goals and ball.

Kick. Jeu comprenant huit figurines mécaniques, plus buts et ballon, 1900.

Kick. Juego en una caja, de principios del siglo XX, con ocho figuras mecánicas, con portería y balón.

Kick. Fußballspiel (nach 1900) mit acht mechanischen Figuren, Toren und Ball.

"Footo Ballo" Table Football game, won Gold Medal in Paris 1908.

Jeu de table de football »Footo Ballo«, Médaille d'or à Paris 1908.

"Footo Ballo" futbolín de mesa, medalla de oro en Paris 1908.

„Footo Ballo". Tischspiel, Goldmedaille Paris 1908.

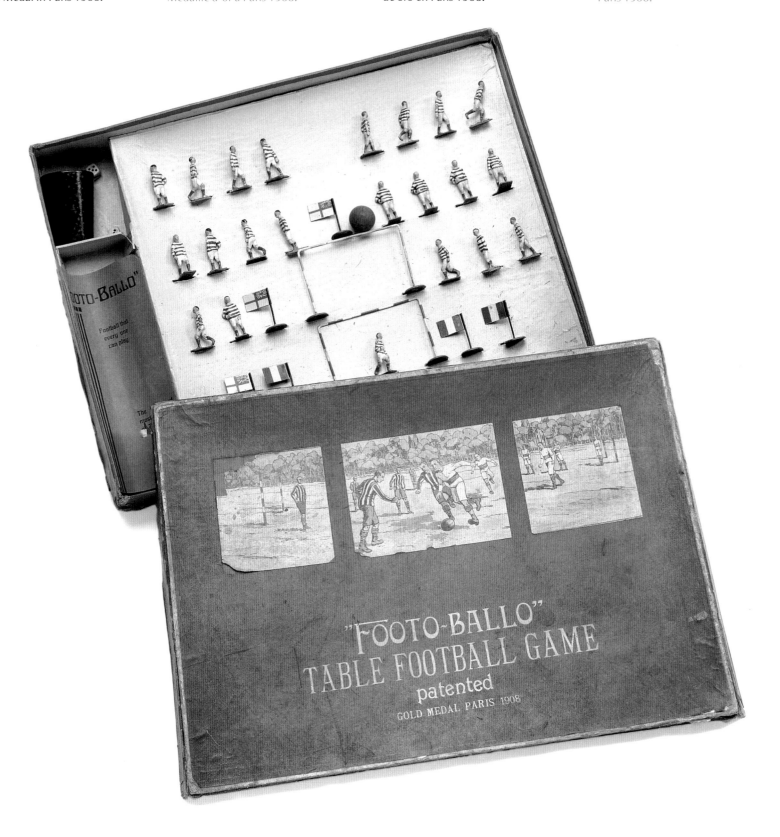

Wibbly-Wob. Edwardian table game.

Wibbly-Wob. Jeu de table de l'époque du roi Edward VII.

Wibbly-Wob. Juego de mesa de la época de Edward VII.

Wibbly-Wob. Tischspiel aus England, um 1910.

Oldest table football game, made in
Preston, England, 1884.

Vieux jeu de table de football réalisé à
Preston en Angleterre, 1884.

El futbolín más antiguo, hecho en
Preston, Inglaterra, 1884.

Das älteste Tisch-Fußballspiel, hergestellt in Preston, England, 1884.

Ding Dong Football. Boxed game with board and counters.

Ding Dong Football. Jeu comprenant tableau et compteurs.

Ding Dong Football. Juego en una caja con tabla y contadores.

Ding Dong Football. Ein Würfelspiel mit Zählmarken.

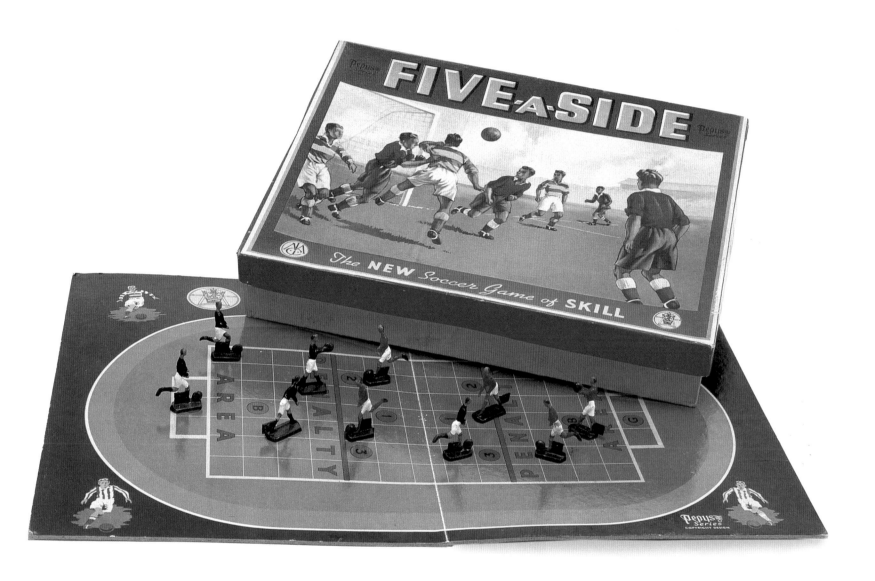

Five-A-Side, British Manufacture, 1950s.

Five-A-Side, manufacture anglaise, 1950.

Five-A-Side, hecho en Gran Bretaña en los años 50.

Five-A-Side. Britisches Spiel aus den fünfziger Jahren.

Foot-It (Made in England early 20th century) within a collage of other games.

Foot-It. Réalisé en Angleterre au début du 20ème siècle, ainsi que d'autres jeux.

Foot-It. Hecho en Inglaterra a principios del siglo XX, junto con otros juegos.

Foot-It. Spiel aus England, Anfang 20. Jahrhundert, dazu einige andere Spiele.

Bema football game, Germany 1920s.

Jeu de football Bema, Allemagne, années1920.

Juego de fútbol Bema, Alemania, de los años 20.

Bema-Fußballspiel aus Deutschland, zwanziger Jahre.

Pin Football. Bagatelle board, in the form of a football pitch, made in England in the 1950s.

Pin Football. Jeu de Bagatelle en forme de terrain de football réalisé en Angleterre dans les années 1950.

Pin Football. Tabla pequeña en forma de un campo de fútbol producido en Inglaterra en los años 50.

Pin Football. Flipper-Spiel in Form eines Fußballfelds, England, fünfziger Jahre.

Soccer Star. Table football game with four metal figures with kicking legs. French, early 20th century.

Soccer Star. Jeu de table avec quatre figurines en métal, le tibia est movible. France, début du 20ème siècle.

Soccer Star. Juego de mesa con cuatro figuras de metal, con una pierna móvil para tirar. Francia, principios del siglo XX.

Soccer Star. Tischspiel mit vier Metall-figuren, das Schußbein beweglich. Frankreich, Anfang 20. Jahrhundert.

TRENCH GOAL FOOTBALL

BRITISH DESIGN   BRITISH MADE

CORNER   BEHIND   THE KAISER   BEHIND   CORNER

COUNT ZEPPELIN   RIGHT BACK   LEFT BACK   VON SANDERS

VON ENVER PASHA

RIGHT HALF   VON DER GOLTZ   VON MOLTKE   LEFT HALF

CENTRE HALF

INSIDE RIGHT   VON HINDENBURG   INSIDE LEFT   VON BULOW

CENTRE FORWARD

VON KLUCK

OUTSIDE RIGHT   VON TERPITZ   OUTSIDE LEFT

LITTLE WILLIE   KICK OFF   REGISTRATION APPLIED FOR

Trench Football. First World War
Game for soldiers in trenches, with
propaganda rules on the back.

Football des tranchées. Jeu de la
première guerre mondiale pour les
soldats dans les tranchées, au dos des
règles de propagande.

Fútbol de fossa. Juego de la primera
guerra mundial para los soldados en las
fossas con frases de propaganda al
dorso.

Trench Football. Britisches Spiel aus
dem Ersten Weltkrieg für Soldaten in
den Schützengräben. Auf der Rückseite
Propaganda-Sprüche.

Early 20th century pub table game with painted wooden players on rods.

Jeu de table de football de pub avec des joueurs en bois peints, début du 20ème siècle.

Futbolín de mesa para tavernas de principios del siglo XX con jugadores de madera pintada, dirigidos por palos.

Britisches Stand-Spiel für Pubs, mit bemalten hölzernen Spielerfiguren auf Achsen, Anfang 20. Jahrhundert.

American football game.

Jeu de football américain.

Juego de fútbol americano.

American Football. Flipper-Spiel aus den USA.

Master Football Game, another arcade game.

Jeu de football des champions. Une autre sorte de jeu d'arcade.

Master Football Game, otro juego de los salones de juegos.

Master Football, ein weiteres Beispiel für Spielhallen-Varianten.

13 The Funny Side
L'humour et le football
La parte graciosa
Die humoristische Seite

Two hundred years ago, European caricaturists were using the brutality of Football games as themes for their political cartoons. It was a safe target. Everyone knew of the blood and thunder of the ancient battles. From the early days of modern Football, the last quarter of the 19th century, cartoonists, illustrators and postcard artists pounced on the new source of an easy laugh.

Many of the visual jokes in the popular magazines and newspapers were at the expense of two central characters who had emerged, the referee and the goalkeeper. Much later, when newspapers were printed in their millions each day, cartoonists who could draw comic reports of big matches on the spot became famous.

Thus, please join in this last chapter presenting some representative examples of "laughing about Football".

Il y a deux cents ans, les caricaturistes européens utilisaient la brutalité du football dans leurs caricatures politiques. C'était une cible facile. Tout le monde connaissait la brutalité et le sang qui coulait lors des anciennes batailles. Depuis les débuts du football moderne à la fin du 19ème siècle, les dessinateurs, illustrateurs et créateurs de cartes postales y trouvèrent une source d'humour bon marché. La plupart de ces blagues que l'on trouve dans la presse de boulevard, se faisaient aux dépens de deux personnages centraux: le juge arbitre et le gardien de but. Bien plus tard, alors que les journaux étaient tirés à des millions d'exemplaires chaque jour, les dessinateurs qui furent capables de rendre compte avec humour des matchs importants devinrent célèbres. C'est pourquoi il serait bon de joindre à ce chapitre quelques illustrations sur «le rire et le football».

Hace 200 años, los caricaturistas europeos se inspiraron en la brutalidad de los juegos de fútbol para sus caricaturas políticas. Era un tiro seguro. Todo el mundo sabía de los elementos sangrientos de las antiguas batallas. Desde los primeros días del fútbol moderno, los últimos 25 años del siglo XIX, los caricaturistas, los ilustradores y diseñadores de postales utilizaron esta nueva fuente de risa fácil. Muchos de las caricaturas en las revistas populares y en los periódicos se hicieron a costa de dos emergentes personajes centrales: el árbitro y el guardameta. Más tarde, cuando los periódicos aumentaron sus tirajes diarios a millones, los caricaturistas deportivos, que cubrían los grandes partidos, se volvieron famosos por sus dibujos.

Ahora, por favor, participe de este capítulo final que muestra algunos ejemplos representativos de "riéndose gracias al fútbol".

Vor 200 Jahren benutzten europäische Karikaturisten die Brutalität beim Fußballspielen als Thema für ihre politischen Zeichnungen. Das war eine sichere Zielscheibe. Jedermann kannte die blutrünstigen Elemente des alten Kampfspiels. Als dann ab 1870 die Geburtsstunde des modernen Fußballs schlug, stürzten sich Karikaturisten, Illustratoren und Postkarten-Künstler auf die neue Quelle eines einfach zu erreichenden Lachens. Viele der Witzbilder in den populären Magazinen und Zeitungen gingen zu Lasten zweier neuentstandener Spezies: des Schiedsrichters und des Torhüters. Als dann viel später die Zeitungen täglich in Millionenauflage erschienen, wurden jene Karikaturisten berühmt, die mit wenigen Strichen komische Szenen der großen Spiele wiederzugeben vermochten.

Genießen Sie also nun das letzte Kapitel des Buches mit repräsentativen Beispielen für „Lachen über Fußball".

Two amusing early 20th century British comic covers.

Deux couvertures de bande dessinées anglaises du début du siècle.

Dos cubiertas graciosas de comics de principios del siglo XX.

Zwei britische Comic-Umschläge, Anfang 20. Jahrhundert.

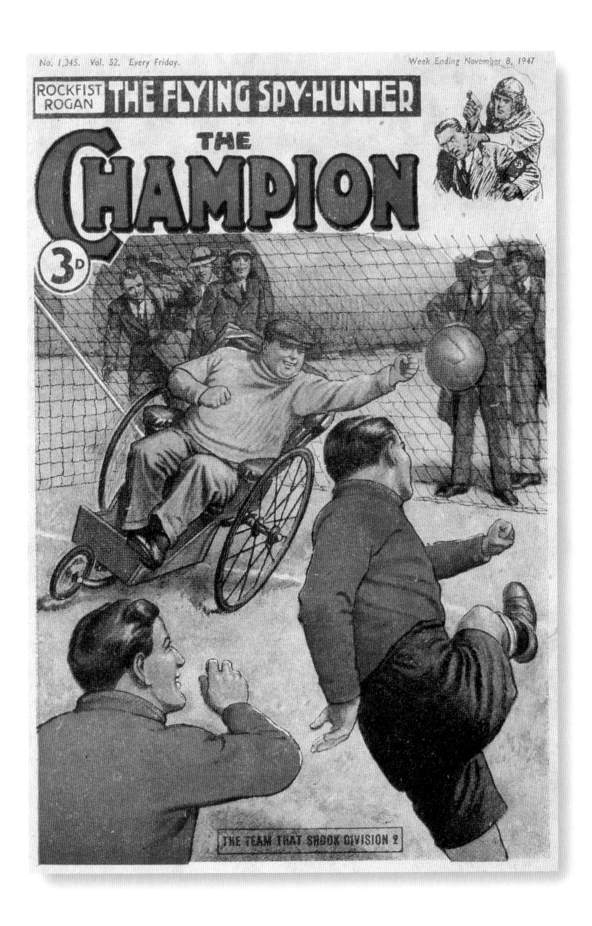

"Billy Lackbeard and Charley Black-beard" (actually the leading politicians Pitt and Scott) "kicking" East India House. Mid-19th century British cartoon.

«Billy Lackbeard and Charley Black-beard» (les politiciens dirigeants de cette époque, Pitt et Scott) jouent au football avec le bâtiment de la East India Company. Caricature britannique, vers 1850.

"Billy Lackbeard and Charley Black-beard" (los políticos dirigentes de aquel entonces, Pitt y Scott) jugando al fútbol con el edificio de la East India Com-pany. Caricatura británica de mediados del siglo XIX.

„Billy Lackbeard and Charley Black-beard" (darstellend die damaligen Spit-zenpolitiker Pitt und Scott) „kicken" mit dem East India House. Britische Karika-tur, Mitte 19. Jahrhundert.

Cover of the French "Le Monde Comi-que", late 19th century. A short-sighted footballer kicks old lady.

Couverture du magazine français «Le Monde Comique», fin du 19ème siècle. Un footballeur donne des coups de pied a une vieille dame.

Cubierta de la revista francesa "Le Monde Comique", fin del siglo XIX. Un futbolista miope da en una señora veja.

Titelseite der französischen „Le Monde Comique", Ende 19. Jahrhundert. Ein kurzsichtiger Spieler trifft eine alte Dame.

'Donald·McGill·

Original watercolour postcard by Donald McGill with his verse: "I once used to think it might injure your brain/ when I looked at you heading the ball./ But now I'm perfectly sure you have none at all/ of course I don't worry at all."

Carte postale d'une aquarelle de Donald McGill avec le couplet: «Autrefois je pensais que tu pourrais nuire à ton intélligence/ quand je t'observais donner des coups de tête au ballon./ Mais maintenant que je suis sûr que tu n'en as pas je ne m'inquiète plus.»

Postal con aquarela de Donald McGill con el siguiente verso: "Antes yo pensaba que podrías dañar a tu inteligencia/ cuando te observaba dando pases de cabeza./ Pero ahora que estoy seguro que no tienes nada semejante/ por supuesto no me preocupa más."

Aquarell-Postkarte von Donald McGill mit den Zeilen: „Einst glaubte ich, es könnte deinem Verstand schaden/ wenn ich dir beim Kopfball zusah./ Aber jetzt, da ich sicher bin, daß du gar keinen hast/ bin ich natürlich nicht mehr besorgt."

Humorous postcards, early 20th century.

Cartes postales humoristiques, début du XXième siècle.

Postales humorísticas, principios del siglo XX.

Humoristische Postkarten, Anfang 20. Jahrhundert.

Humorous postcards by Tom Browne, early 20th century.

Cartes postales humoristiques de Tom Browne, début du XXième siècle.

Postales humorísticas de Tom Browne, principios del siglo XX.

Humoristische Postkarten von Tom Browne, Anfang 20. Jahrhundert.

Crowd scene by "G. J." (unidentified), early 20th century watercolour. A lad seems to be protesting to a neighbour that he has stepped on his chewing gum.

Scène de foule d'après «G. J.» (non identifié), aquarelle du début du 20ème siècle. Un jeune homme semble se plaindre auprès d'un voisin.

Escena de muchedumbre de "G. J." acuarela de principios del siglo XX. Un muchacho parece regañar a un vecino, que ha pisado su chicle.

Aquarell von „G. J.", Anfang 20. Jahrhundert. Ein junger Bursche beschwert sich bei einem Nachbarn, weil dieser auf seinen Kaugummi getreten ist.

"Yur, move thee gurt feet, bolzt, thee bist treadin' on my chewingum!"

"Shoot, shoot …" Cartoon for the
London "Evening Standard", 1970s.

«Tire, tire …», bande dessinée pour le
journal londonien «Evening Standard»,
1970.

"Tira, tira…" Dibujo para el "Evening
Standard" en Londres, años 70.

„Schieß doch …!" Karikatur für den
Londoner „Evening Standard",
ca. 1975.

A large comic "Valentine" printed in
the 1900s.

Bande dessinée «Valentine» publiée
au début du siècle.

Un comic largo "Valentine" impreso
a principios del siglo XX.

„Valentine"-Comic, um 1900.

Finga-Foota. World War I table football game with 6 cardboard cut-outs of famous personalities, which were attached to the hands of "players" by elastic bands. Also rubber "boots" and celluloid ball. Of course everyone knows Charlie Chaplin.

Finga-Foota. Football de table de la première guerre mondiale avec six personnages connus découpés dans du carton. Ces personnages étaient attachés aux mains des joueurs par des élastiques. Il y avait également des chaussures en caoutchouc et un ballon en celluloïde. Bien entendu, tout le monde reconnaît Charlie Chaplin.

Finga-Foota. Futbolín de mesa de la primera guerra mundial con 6 recortes de personajes famosos atados a las manos de los jugadores por cintas elásticas. También botas de goma y un balón de celuloide. Por supuesto todos conocen a Charlie Chaplin.

Finga-Foota. Tischspiel aus dem Ersten Weltkrieg mit 6 Spielfiguren berühmter Persönlichkeiten, die mit Gummis an den Fingern der „Spieler" befestigt werden, dazu Gummi„schuhe" und ein Zelluloid-Ball. Natürlich kennt ein jeder Charlie Chaplin.

Ashtray with John Hassall figure of a footballer. The head is a moveable football.

Cendrier de John Hassall avec la figurine d'un footballeur. La tête est un ballon mouvant.

Cenizero de John Hassall con la figura de un futbolista. La cabeza es un balón movible.

Aschenbecher mit Fußballerfigur von John Hassall, der Kopf in Form eines abnehmbaren Fußballs.

Contents
Contenu
Indice
Inhalt

We support the worldwide work of the SOS Children's Villages,
the partner of FIFA, with proceeds from this book.

Acec le produit de la vente de ce livre, nous assistons les
Villages d'Enfants SOS, le partenaire de la FIFA, dans leur travail.

Con el beneficio de la venta de este libro apoyamos la labor
mundial de las Aldeas Infantiles SOS, el socio de la FIFA.

Aus dem Verkaufserlös dieses Buches unterstützen wir die
Arbeit der SOS-Kinderdörfer, des Partners der FIFA.

FIFA FOR SOS CHILDREN'S VILLAGES

FIFA POUR LES VILLAGES D'ENFANTES SOS

FIFA PARA ALDEAS INFANTES SOS

FIFA FÜR SOS - KINDERDÖRFER

Die Deutsche Bibliothek – CIP-Einheitsaufnahme

1000 years of football: FIFA Museum Collection = 1000 ans de football
= 1000 años de fútbol = 1000 Jahre Fußball / [hrsg. von SPI Group und der FIFA].
– Berlin: Ed. q, 1996.
   ISBN 3-86124-325-3
NE: Federation Internationale de Football Association; Thousand years of
football; Mille ans de football; Mil años de fútbol; Tausend Jahre Fußball

Presented by SPI Group, White Plains, N. Y., USA,
in cooperation with FIFA, Zurich, Switzerland.

Introduction by Clive Toye
Text by Harry Langton
Photography by Michael Ammann
Special thanks to Jason Silverstein and Dr. Frank D. Braun

Copyright © 1996 by edition q, Verlags-GmbH, Berlin - Chicago - Tokio

All images Copyright © 1996 by FIFA Museum Collection™.

Art Direction: Atelier Höpfner-Thoma, Munich, Germany
Colour separations: Color Exchange Inc., Chatsworth, CA, USA
Printing and Binding: Bosch-Druck, Landshut, Germany
Printed in Germany

ISBN 3-86124-335-0 (Regular edition, Hardcover)
       3-86124-325-3 (Softcover)   3-86124-330-X (Luxury edition)